Mastering

Study Skills

Macmillan Master Series

Accounting
Arabic
Astronomy
Australian History
Background to Business
Banking
Basic Management
Biology
British Politics
Business Communication
Business Law
Business Microcomputing
C Programming
Catering Science
Catering Theory
Chemistry
COBOL Programming
Commerce
Computer Programming
Computers
Economic and Social History
Economics
Electrical Engineering
Electronics
English as a Foreign Language
English Grammar
English Language
English Literature
Financial Accounting
French 1
French 2
German 1
German 2

Hairdressing
Human Biology
Italian 1
Italian 2
Japanese
Keyboarding
Marketing
Mathematics
Modern British History
Modern European History
Modern World History
Nutrition
Office Practice
Pascal Programming
Philosophy
Physics
Practical Writing
Principles of Accounts
Psychology
Restaurant Service
Science
Secretarial Procedures
Social Welfare
Sociology
Spanish 1
Spanish 2
Spreadsheets
Statistics
Statistics with your Microcomputer
Study Skills
Typewriting Skills
Word Processing

Mastering

Study Skills

Second Edition

Richard Freeman

MACMILLAN

First published 1982 by
THE MACMILLAN PRESS LTD
Houndmills, Basingstoke, Hampshire RG21 2XS
and London
Companies and representatives
throughout the world

ISBN 0–333–54929–5

A catalogue record for this book is available
from the British Library.

Printed in China

First edition reprinted seven times
Second edition 1991
10   9   8   7   6   5   4   3   2
00   99   98   97   96   95   94   93   92

Contents

List of figures

⬡ Preface

As modern life increases in complexity, all of us are drawn into learning an ever wider range of topics. No longer are we satisfied with 'reading, writing and arithmetic'. We find ourselves learning the sciences, languages, business subjects, nutrition, health, etc., etc.

But what is the one thing we rarely learn about? Learning. This omission strikes me as odd. The more important learning becomes to us all, the more we need to understand how we learn. This book sets out to help you gain that understanding.

The theme of this book is that each one of us learns in slightly different ways so the key to success is finding out what works for you. Throughout the book you will find out more about how you have learnt in the past. It helps you answer questions like: What things do you remember easily? What things do you find hard to remember? How well do the notes you make work for you? How much information can you extract from a chapter of a book?

Once you know what has worked well for you in the past, then you can go on to improve on these methods. By the end of the book you will have built up a strong range of study skills which help you learn more effectively in less time. You will have learnt about learning.

Your improved skills will include: making realistic plans, keeping yourself motivated, how to check your progress, finding just the information that you want, keeping really effective notes, improving your memory and producing better-written work.

Above all I hope this book will help you to become more confident in planning and directing your own learning. Of course you will still use tutors and lecturers, you will still ask others for help, but this time you will be in charge, getting exactly the help you need.

So why not start now with Chapter 1, which helps you to find out what you really want to get out of study?

RICHARD FREEMAN

The author and publishers are grateful to Oxford County Newspapers for permission to reproduce the photograph on page 73.

1 Getting started

1.1 Introduction

Most of us spend years studying at school but are never taught anything about study itself. A few succeed despite this handicap; most do not. Overwhelmingly, people leave school lacking confidence in their ability to learn. This book is for anyone in that position.

It is not a book about how to become cleverer but a book about how to use the brains that you have more effectively. It sets out to show you that success in study is not an accident. It comes from using effective learning techniques. It also comes from exploring how you learn, observing what works well for you and what does not. At the end of this book you will have:

- found out what you learn easily and what with difficulty;
- tried out ways of making the difficult items easier to learn;
- found out what you remember easily and what with difficulty;
- tried out ways of making the items that you find difficult to remember easier to remember;
- tried out lots of ways to make effective notes that are easy to learn from;
- established realistic study times and methods to keep to them;
- acquired many more specific skills.

Most of all this book aims to increase your confidence in your learning skills. If it succeeds then you will be convinced that your study achievements depend on what you do for yourself, not on what others do to you. You will appreciate that what matters is not how you are taught but how you learn. We start by looking at how successful you now are in your learning.

1.2 Why are you studying?

People generally achieve what really matters to them. The rest is often left undone. However busy your day, you probably still find time to do the things you want to do. However idle your day, it passes without you ever completing the chores.

1

Why do some things get done, but not others? It is all to do with motivation – the forces which drive you to want to do one thing rather than another – but before you can look at your motivation, you need a clear idea of your target. Few people study for study's sake and I shall assume that you too have some more concrete goal in mind: something which you want to achieve through study. In this section you will begin to identify what your goals might be as a first step to being more in control of your learning.

Activity 1.1   Why are you studying?

Tick off the reasons below which match your reasons for study. Note down any additional reasons that apply to you.

Reason	*Tick if this applies to you*
1. To prove to myself that I can do it.	✓
2. Because the subject interests me.	✓
3. To qualify to get on another course.	
4. To gain a qualification.	
5. To get a better job.	✓
6. My parents/employer insist that I study.	
7. Other.	✓

To become a better teacher
To publish

These reasons fall into three groups. Reasons 1 and 2 are personal reasons and are their own reward. If you have ticked 1 or 2 (or even better, 1 and 2), then you probably feel pretty determined about your study. You may have problems – you probably do if you are reading this book – but you have the will to overcome them. Ticking 3, 4 or 5 still shows that your study aims are important to you but the reward is what comes later, not the study itself. So, you may find studying a drag because that ultimate reward is so far away. Finally, if you ticked 6 then you are probably a reluctant learner. You do not want to study but someone else is in a position to force you to do so.

As you will see when I discuss motivation in more depth, there are lots of ways to increase it. I will look at one approach now since it is the basis on which everything else in this book is built. Quite simply, successful study depends on your study being important to you. Unless you can make it important to you, unless you can make it enjoyable and rewarding, your study will remain a boring chore.

┌─ **Activity 1.2   I really want to . . .** ──────────────────────┐

If there is nothing that you really want to get out of your study, you might as well give up now – it is your life and you should be making the choices. Meanwhile I will suppose that you do have something that you wish to achieve. Now is your chance to identify those goals.

Tick those goals that form part of what you want to get out of your study.

Goal	Tick if this applies to you
1. I want to enjoy studying . . .	✓
2. I want to understand the work which I am doing on . . . ME	✓
3 I want to pass the test on . . .	
4. I want my study of .ME. to be more relevant to my job.	✓
5. I want the free time that I will have when I pass this course.	
6. I want the more rewarding life that I will have when I get a better job.	✓
7. I want . . . (complete with your own reason) *to find out where my research talents lie*	✓

└──┘

First, I hope that however negative your answers to Activity 1.1 were, you have found something more positive in Activity 1.2. Perhaps you ticked 1. This shows that you do believe that the process of study could be enjoyable in itself. It can be, and I will look at some ways of making it so later in this book.

If you ticked 2 or 3, then you are beginning to break down your long-term goal into some more immediately achievable short-term goals. The smaller a task, the easier it is to achieve, so ticking 2 or 3 is good progress.

If you have ticked 1, 2 or 3 then you have already found something that is important to you to achieve. But if you have only ticked 4, 5 or 6, then you may still find it useful to look for something more immediate to achieve. You will do that later in this chapter.

By now you should have explored your reasons for study in some depth. You should be clear as to whether you have found reasons that are important to you. I hope that you have because they are the key to your success.

1.3   What do you learn best?

We do not all learn in the same way. Much of this book is about helping you to find out which methods work for you and then improving on those methods. For example, some people learn best through discussion; others learn through quiet work alone. Some like to learn the theory first and then look for examples to illustrate it; others need the examples first before they feel ready for the theory. There is a very simple way to find out how you learn best: to reflect on your own past experience.

Activity 1.3   Easy to learn/hard to learn

a) Write down five to ten things which you have found easy to learn. Try to choose examples that cover as many types of learning as possible, e.g. driving a car or learning French verbs.

b)   Now write down five to ten things that you have found very difficult to learn. Again, choose examples that are as varied as possible.

To make sense of your easy-to-learn/hard-to-learn lists you have to analyse what type of learning is involved in each case and then see what the pattern tells you about yourself.

Take each of the items in your two lists and try to fit them into one or more of the following categories.

Category	Easy to learn	Hard to learn
Facts (e.g. names, poetry)	*quotes* *Vocab*	*Names & details* *Dates, places* *Factual info*
Physical skills (e.g. driving, piano playing)	*Cooking* *Playing recorder* *? Word processing* *Bike riding*	*Driving*
Concepts (e.g. voltage, negative numbers, harmony)	*? Fiction writing*	*Literary theory* *Logical thinking*

(handwritten margin notes:)

a) word processing
quotes
Italian vocab
Cooking
IhS studies

b) Names &
details
Logical
thinking
Driving car
Languages
Exp. Comp.
Lit theory

Rules (e.g. formulae)	*Basic languages Highway Code Recipes*	*Advanced languages esp: comprehension*
Application (e.g. problem solving, writing essays)	*MS studies up to a point*	*Problem Solving Writing essays*

There is no simple conclusion to draw from this activity, but its results will become more and more meaningful to you as you work through this book. However I can make some general comments with which you can compare your response.

Most people find facts hard to learn. That is because knowing one fact is no help in learning another. Facts are isolated bits of information which rarely fit the patterns of our minds. So, if you have put facts under the 'hard-to-learn' heading, you are like most of us. Later in this book I will look at some ways to get around this difficulty of learning facts.

On the other hand, most people find at least some physical skills easy to learn – just look at how many millions of people learn to ride a bicycle or to drive a car. Physical skills are easy to learn because, as we attempt them, the result gives us feedback which we automatically use to improve our performance. Humans are natural physical-skill learners.

If you have put 'concepts' on your 'easy-to-learn' list, then you probably have excellent study skills. But many people find learning concepts difficult and wonder why this is so. Often it is because the way in which they have been taught has encouraged memorising the concepts instead of understanding them. By the end of this book, you will have mastered the difference between these two approaches and should be finding it much easier to learn concepts.

Rules are much like concepts in their learning difficulty. A rule will appear difficult if either you do not understand the concepts behind it, or you have not practised using the rule in a wide enough range of circumstances.

Finally the practical application of what you have learnt often causes difficulties for learners. The cause is simple enough – we will come to cures later: application is based on a thorough understanding of the concepts and rules of your subject. Given that the facts, rules and concepts cause enough problems themselves, no wonder application is difficult.

1.4   How do you learn best?

You have looked at what you can learn most easily and at what gives you problems. To complete the picture, you need to work out which learning methods work best for you.

Activity 1.4   How you learn

For this activity you will use the same list of five to ten 'easy-to-learn' and five to ten 'hard-to-learn' items which you compiled for Activity 1.3. This time you are going to consider the method which enabled you to succeed or fail in your learning. Take each of your items and place them in one of the groups below.

Learning method	Easy to learn by this method	Hard to learn by this method
Group a Learning by heart	quotes vocab recipes	Lit theory
Group b Watching TV Listening to the radio Listening to a lecturer	Fiction writing dramatised Lit Crit	Written style Lit theory
Group c Video under my control Audio tape under my control Textbook		
Group d Lecture with question/discussion		

Group e In a group Role-play		
Group f Trying it for myself Applying it to lots of problems Explaining it to others Doing a project Solving a real problem On the job		

I can only guess at the pattern of your responses to Activity 1.4 and it is quite impossible for me to discuss every possible combination of answers. So I am going to have to make some fairly broad generalisations, confident that most of you will recognise something of the pattern of your responses. Moreover, I can confidently say that the more items you consider for this activity, and the wider their range, then the nearer you will come to the pattern in Figure 1.1.

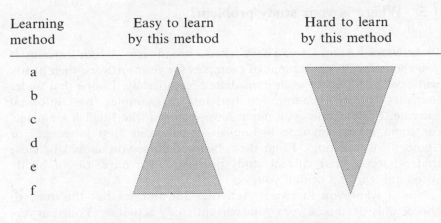

Learning method	Easy to learn by this method	Hard to learn by this method
a		
b		
c		
d		
e		
f		

Figure 1.1   Patterns of learning difficulty

Why should this be so? Look at the list of learning methods, noting the groupings (a) to (f). (a) is trying to learn without any understanding – the hardest way to learn anything. Methods (b) to (f) involve increasing levels of activity on your part and increasing opportunities to get feedback. Remember that feedback tells you how you are doing so that you can make adjustments to improve your learning. Crudely, the learning methods in the list are ranked from 'most passive' to 'most active' as shown in Figure 1.2. In other words, the more active a learning method is, the more you will learn.

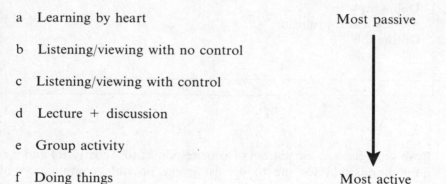

a   Learning by heart

b   Listening/viewing with no control

c   Listening/viewing with control

d   Lecture + discussion

e   Group activity

f   Doing things

Figure 1.2   The activity level of different learning methods

1.5   Where is your study problem?

In Activities 1.3 and 1.4 you have taken a broad view of your learning. If you chose a really wide range of examples for your answers, then plenty will have been outside your immediate area of study. I hope that under the 'easy-to-learn' heading you had lots of examples from informal learning. For example, you might have included 'the English language' (or some other language if English is not your first language) or 'football' or 'cooking'. From these two activities, you should be clear that, whatever your current study problems, you have lots of highly successful learning behind you.

Now I want you to repeat Activities 1.3 and 1.4 but this time to choose only examples from your current study activities. Your answers will appear in Activities 1.5 and 1.6 below.

Activity 1.5   Easy-to-learn/hard-to-learn in your study

Write down five to ten things which you have found easy to learn in your current course of study. Try to choose examples that cover as many types of learning as possible.

Now write down five to ten things that you have found very difficult to learn. Again, choose examples that are as varied as possible.

As before, take each of the items in your two lists and try to fit them into one or more of the following categories.

Category	Easy to learn	Hard to learn
Facts (e.g. names, poetry)		
Physical skills (e.g. driving, piano playing)		
Concepts (e.g. voltage, negative numbers, harmony)		
Rules (e.g. formulae)		
Application (e.g. problem solving, writing essays)		

You have a clear list of what you find difficult to learn in your current subject. But it is more than a random list of topics: it is a carefully categorised list which tells you the type (or types) of learning that are causing you problems. This list is so important in terms of how you use the rest of this book, that I suggest that you summarise it in a few sentences.

So, if 'facts' are your main problem, you will from now on be concentrating on using the rest of this book to help with fact-learning. To complete your agenda for action, you need to consider the learning methods which you have been using. The next activity helps you to do this.

Activity 1.6   How you have tried to learn difficult topics

From Activity 1.5, take the items that you find hard to learn in your current study area, and record below the study methods that you have used to try and learn them.

Learning methods used on your 'hard-to-learn' topics

Learning method	Topic
Group a Learning by heart	
Group b Watching TV Listening to the radio Listening to a lecturer	

Group c
Video under my
  control
Audio tape under
  my control
Textbook	

Group d Lecture with question/discussion	

Group e In a group Role-play		

Group f
Trying it for myself
Applying it to lots
  of problems
Explaining it to
  others
Doing a project
Solving a real problem
On the job		

Remember that this last table shows what did not work for you. From Activities 1.3, 1.4, 1.5 and 1.6 you should be able to make a good guess at which learning methods you are neglecting. Record these here.

1.6   Setting goals

Quite often, formal education encourages you to leave all the planning of your study to your tutors. You then become the passive recipient of instructions from your tutor: 'Learn this', 'Learn that', Write this' and 'Write that'. In these circumstances it is difficult to see where you are going and impossible to use your time and energy to best effect. Your learning needs are unique to you. Only you know which topics you find easy and so can skip. Only you know which learning methods work best for you. Only you can decide what is an achievable goal for you over the next week, two weeks, month or whatever. This section begins to put you in charge of those decisions.

A key part of 'getting started' is setting yourself clear and realistic goals. First, here is an activity to help you see how good your current goal-setting is.

Activity 1.7   Your current goals

To get the most out of this (and the next) activity, you need to be really honest with yourself – only you lose if you are not.

Check in your own current written plans what goals you have set yourself for your current study programme. Write these down below. Remember, it is the plans that you have already made, not the plans that you wish you had made.

Your current written goals

Time period	Goals
Next two weeks	
Next month	
Next three months	
Next six months	
Next year	

If you have been able to write down clear goals (like 'complete my second continuous assessment item' or 'reach 40 wpm in my typing') then you already know how to set yourself goals. If your goals are vague (like 'get halfway through the syllabus' or 'get better at algebra') then you need to do more work on goals. Read on.

Goals will only be effective if they satisfy two criteria:

● they must be realistic;
● they must be clear cut.

First, consider what 'realistic' means. If you set yourself goals that you know that you cannot achieve, you will soon give up any effort to reach them. They will have failed as goals. (Goals are meant to be scored, not missed.)

Second, consider what makes a 'clear cut' goal. It needs to be something which you can clearly say you have or have not achieved. So 'Write a 1500 word essay on . . .' or 'Complete two past exam papers' are good examples of goals. You can always tell whether or not you have achieved them.

Activity 1.0   Setting yourself goals

Now try setting some goals for the next three months. Make sure that, in each case, the goal is something that you will be able to clearly say has or has not been achieved.

1.7   Setting objectives

Setting objectives is much like setting goals, but at a more detailed level. Goals are usually too big to achieve in one – or even a few – study sessions. Objectives may be achievable in a week or so. They are the stepping stones towards goals.

Whenever you sit down to a study session, you need a clear target of what you wish to achieve. This will:

● concentrate your efforts towards the one thing that you consider important;
● give you a sense of achievement at the end of your session;
● show you how you are progressing towards your goals.

Like goals, objectives need to be clear-cut. You have to know whether you have or have not achieved them. So, 'learn about cells' is far too vague. 'Learn the names of the parts of a cell and be able to draw and label a diagram from memory' is a good, precise objective. The output (your labelled diagram) is something which you clearly do – or do not – achieve.

Activity 1.9   Check your objective setting

In this activity you are going to review some objectives that you have set yourself in the past in order to see how well you phrase them. Write in the first column below five things you have recently set yourself to learn. Then consider whether these objectives were precise enough to act as a real measure of your progress. If they were not, work out a more precise wording for your objectives, putting it in the second column.

Your sample objectives	*Your more precise phrasings*
1.	
2.	
3.	
4.	
5.	

By now it should be clear to you that you can use goals and objectives to break down a large task (say your whole course) into small enough chunks for you to tackle. What you do is very similar to the method which I used to write this book. First I wrote a general description which set out the purpose and general character of the book (my 'course'). Then I wrote a description of what each chapter would cover (my 'goals' – one per chapter). Finally I split each chapter into sections with their activities (my 'objectives'). So, my plan can be pictured as Figure 1.3.

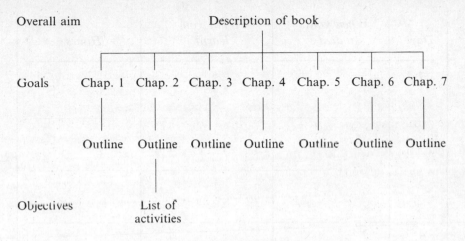

Figure 1.3   Plan for book

Activity 1.10   Splitting a goal into objectives

Take one of your goals from Activity 1.8 and subdivide it into objectives. Try to choose objectives that are detailed enough to be achievable at a single study session.

1.8   Plans and timetables

Now that you have subdivided your course into goals – and begun working out detailed objectives – you can start to consider how to timetable your study. This is both very simple and very hard. Simple because anyone can fill in grand plans on a timetable. Hard because all of us are wildly optimistic about what we can achieve in a given time. So the best place to start is with an assessment of what is realistic for you.

Activity 1.11   How much study do you do?

As with the other activities, the more honest you are with yourself, the more you will get out of this activity. Complete the table below for the last seven days, ending with yesterday.

Day	When you studied	What you learnt	Hours
7			
6			
5			
4			
3			
2			
1			
TOTAL FOR WEEK			

What can you learn from this? Four main things:

● which seem to be the best times for study;
● how effectively you use your study time;
● the duration of a typical study period for you;
● how much study you can fit into a week.

So, if your analysis showed that you spent ten hours last week on study, how realistic is it to plan for 15 hours per week in future? If you found that you achieved most of your learning in morning sessions, but the evening ones were unsuccessful, how sensible is it to plan for more evening study?

Activity 1.12   Framework for your timetable

Keeping to complete honesty and realism, use the results of Activity 1.11 to complete the following:

- Your best study times are:
- Your worst study times are:
- Your shortest useful study period is:
- Your longest useful study period is:
- Your maximum number of study hours per week is:

What hours does your course require?

Your timetable analysis so far has been based on your actual study patterns. There is a good reason for this: it is remarkably difficult to change personal study routines. Any workable timetable that you create will owe much more to what you are like than to some imaginary ideal of how you ought to be. However, to be realistic, you will have to compare your typical study pattern with the demands of your course. That is your next activity.

Activity 1.13   What does your course demand?

Compare the number of hours required by your course with your typical weekly number.

	Example	*Your figures*
Course requires	150 hrs	
Your hours available/week	5 hrs	
Your course will take	30 weeks	

If your course has no fixed end-date, then you are free to decide whether you are happy with your figures. In my example above, I might really want to finish the course within 20 weeks. Clearly I cannot do that at the rate of five hours per week so I have to decide whether I am willing to increase my study time to 7½ hours per week.

I will suppose that you too have found that your current rate of working will not enable you to complete the course by the chosen date. What can you do? You could simply calculate – as I did above – how many hours a week you will need to complete the course on time. But would this be realistic? Only you will know. If you are in doubt about the realism of this approach, consider some of the options open to you:

- omit some parts of the course;
- negotiate a later completion date;
- negotiate to take the course in stages;
- extend your study hours a little bit more, but not more than you can easily manage.

Drawing up the timetable

At last you can now draw up a timetable. You may wonder why I have taken so long to get around to this. Quite simply, because most of us fill in timetables with little thought to the commitment that we are making. The last three activities should have helped you to take a realistic view of your own situation.

Activity 1.14   Completing the timetable

Fill in the blank timetable in Figure 1.4 opposite to show when you are going to study. Complete it in the following order:

- Block out fixed events, e.g. sleep, work, meals.
- Mark at least two days of the week as 'study free' days – everyone needs proper rest, relaxation and exercise.
- On the other five days, timetable your planned study hours (from Activity 1.13) at your best study times (from Activity 1.12) as evenly as possible across the five days.
- If you still have a good few blocks of spare time do not be tempted to fill them up. Remember Activity 1.11!

1.9   Study periods

How you use each of your study periods can make a lot of difference to how successful they are. You can probably tell that from your past experience.

	Sun	Mon	Tues	Wed	Thur	Fri	Sat
0.00							
1.00							
2.00							
3.00							
4.00							
5.00							
6.00							
7.00							
8.00							
9.00							
10.00							
11.00							
12.00							
13.00							
14.00							
15.00							
16.00							
17.00							
18.00							
19.00							
20.00							
21.00							
22.00							
23.00							

Figure 1.4 Blank timetable

Activity 1.15   How you use your study periods ────────

In the table below are a variety of ways in which you might use study periods. For each of your study periods in the seven days finishing yesterday, classify the way that you used these periods.

Method of study					*Period*					
	1	*2*	*3*	*4*	*5*	*6*	*7*	*8*	*9*	*10*
1 Read (no other activity)										
2 Copied out from books or notes										
3 Tackled a variety of tasks										
4 Worked until you were bored/tired										
5 Worked for planned length of time										
6 Set yourself an objective and worked until you mastered it										

Now rank the six approaches according to how successful they have been for you.

I imagine that your rating is not very different from mine. There is no 'right' answer, but most people rank the order something like:

Most successful   6, 4 and 5
Least successful   3, 1 and 2

Here are some of the reasons behind this order, working upwards from the least successful to the most successful.

Look back to Activity 1.4. There you explored the link between ease of learning and method of learning. The more active (in the sense of *using* what is to be learnt) a method is, the greater success it generally has. With this knowledge behind you, it is not hard to predict that the most passive of the approaches to a study period (i.e. reading and copying out) are likely to be the least successful.

Of the methods listed in Activity 1.15, method 3 (tackling a variety of tasks) rarely works and for two reasons. First, you do not spend long enough on any one task to make any progress with it. Second, the differing tasks tend to 'interfere' with each other: as you try to learn the second item, it stops the first from being fully absorbed by your brain.

Method 4 (working until you are tired or bored) is usually ineffective because both tiredness and boredom inhibit learning. They are warning signals from your brain that it is not concentrating on the task you have set it.

With luck the method 5 (working for a planned time) will work – but only through luck. Suppose the length of study was too short to learn the item on which you were working. You stop. Then, because you never mastered the topic, it fades much more rapidly from your brain than it would had it been mastered.

So, finally we come to method 6 (working at one task until it is mastered). This is generally the most effective approach, but with an odd twist. If you re-learn (or re-practice) something which you have just mastered, the extra learning produces even better retention of what you are learning. This effect is called 'over-learning'.

That is all a fairly lengthy analysis of how you might use individual study periods. If I add one more point, you will be in a position to plan your study for maximum effect. The one additional point concerns how long study periods should be – see Activity 1.16.

Activity 1.16   Length of study periods

In this activity you are going to analyse the effectiveness of different length study periods. Complete the activity for all your study periods over the last seven days. When you assess the effectiveness of each period, ask yourself whether you could have achieved as much in a shorter time.

Length of study period	*Number of periods*	*Your assessment of their effectiveness*
0 to 10 minutes		
11 to 20 minutes		
21 to 40 minutes		
41 to 60 minutes		
61 to 90 minutes		
91 to 120 minutes		
121 minutes or more		

Again there are no right answers but there are some general principles which show up in people's study patterns. These are:

- Very short (say up to 10 minutes) periods are ineffective. Our minds seem to need a warming-up period of 5 to 10 minutes during which nothing much is learnt.
- Very long periods (say 90 minutes and over) tend to induce tiredness and boredom.

So most people find that their study periods are best kept to between 20 and 90 minutes. You will find which works best for you.

1.10   Conclusion

You now have all the information which you need in order to plan your study sessions for maximum effect. In summary you need to design each period:

- to fit one complete learning objective
- to allow a bit of extra time for 'over-learning'
- not too short – say 20 minutes minimum
- not too long – say 90 minutes maximum.

② Keeping going

2.1 Introduction

This chapter is all about motivation. When we do something of our own free will, then we must have a reason for doing it. That is our motivation. It is impossible for an observer to know what another person's motivation is. Imagine that you see someone running along a street. Why might they be doing so? I can think of several possible reasons straight away:

- to get (or keep) fit;
- because the runner enjoys running;
- because the runner wants to get somewhere quickly;
- to impress the locality.

On the whole we do not think about our motives very much, even though they are what drive us to do almost everything that we do. Sometimes we are forced to consider our motives when someone questions them. 'You're only doing that because . . .' At that point we are forced to consider whether we have a good or a bad motive. You will not have to face such deep issues in this chapter. What concerns us is not whether your motives are good or bad, but whether you have found an effective way of motivating yourself to study. We will start by considering what sort of things motivate you.

Activity 2.1   What you like doing

Write down ten things that are really rewarding or enjoyable for you to do. Choose as wide a range as possible, covering personal life, family life and work life.

23

2.2   Exploring your motivation

Now you are going to look more closely at what it is that gives you satisfaction in these activities. To do this, you need to be able to distinguish between two types of satisfaction: intrinsic and extrinsic.

- **Intrinsic satisfaction** occurs when the task itself is its own reward – it is not done for any future benefit. So, we get intrinsic satisfaction out of: laughing at a joke, drinking a glass of water when we are thirsty or (for some people) running.
- **Extrinsic satisfaction** occurs when an outcome associated with the task is the reward. The task itself may even be unpleasant but we still do it for its future benefit. Examples of tasks which are extrinsically rewarding are: having an aching tooth removed, cleaning the house, (for some people) running.

Notice that any task is capable of giving intrinsic or extrinsic satisfaction – it all depends on the individual. So, some people hate running but do it to keep fit. For them the reward (being fit) is extrinsic to the task (running). For others, running is in itself enjoyable and so gives intrinsic satisfaction.

Activity 2.2   What gives you satisfaction?

Go back to the list of things that you like doing which you wrote down in Activity 2.1. Identify what, for you, are the intrinsic and extrinsic rewards in each case. Some tasks may yield both types of reward.

The balance that you have between intrinsic and extrinsic rewards may simply reflect the tasks that you chose for the activity or it may reflect the general balance for you. Some people ignore long-term rewards and concentrate on tasks that have short-term rewards. Others will persevere with tasks that have little intrinsic satisfaction but bring worthwhile long-term rewards.

The more you are motivated by extrinsic rewards, the easier you are likely to find study – especially study where someone else has set down what is to be learnt. Most study is undertaken for its long-term rewards – such as gaining a qualification – rather than for immediate enjoyment. The less that long-term rewards motivate you, the more you have to find ways of enjoying the immediate process of study.

Activity 2.3   Rating your motivation

Your study programme will involve some long-term aim (like passing an exam or gaining a qualification). Rate this for motivation as compared to the short-term process of study.

Long-term aim

Does not motivate   __   __   __   __   __   Highly motivating
at all
$$-2 \quad -1 \quad 0 \quad 1 \quad 2$$

The process of study

Does not motivate   __   __   __   __   __   Highly motivating
at all
$$-2 \quad -1 \quad 0 \quad 1 \quad 2$$

Analysing your scores

3 or 4   You are highly motivated. Motivation should not be a problem for you.

0 to 2   Middling motivation which you probably feel is not enough to keep you going. The rest of this chapter will help with this.

−1 or −2   Motivation is clearly a problem for you. This chapter could be very important to you.

−3 or −4   Motivation is a serious problem for you. At the end of this chapter you will need to assess whether you really ought to be tackling your course at all. Maybe you have other more pressing needs or interests.

2.3   When do you grind to a halt?

Unless you are exceptional, you will have found times in your study when you have felt that you cannot go on or are stuck in some way. Reviewing such situations can help you to see their causes and so to take action to prevent or overcome future occurrences.

Activity 2.4   When have you got stuck?

Try to identify up to ten occasions (from any study at any time) when you felt that you were making no progress. Number the items 1 to 10.

Now try to match what you think was the problem against the following list. Write in the number of your problem from your list above into the table below.

	Cause	Your items
A	Did not understand previous material	
B	Pace too fast	
	Teaching too abstract	
	Badly taught	
C	Low marks	
	Poor achievement	
D	Boring	
	Could not see the relevance to me or my course	
E	Other (write in your own reasons)	

You will see that I have suggested eight possible reasons but have placed them in five groups. I will comment on the possible causes in their groups.

Group A identifies the cause of your problem as being prior to the topic that ground you to a halt. Learning almost any topic depends on learning something else first. To take an extreme example, most school and college courses assume that you can read. If you could not read, you would make no progress on such a course. To take some less extreme examples, you could not learn about harmony if you did not understand musical scales. Nor could you learn quadratic equations if you had not mastered linear equations first. The cure to problems in this group is usually simple: halt your study of the topic that is causing a problem and go back to learn the missing prior topic.

Group B is a set of three causes which are all about the way that you are being taught. You may think that there is nothing that you can do about this, but there is. First, you – or, better, you and some colleagues – could try explaining your position to your teacher. Often teachers are quite willing to adjust the way that they teach, but never get any feedback to help them to do so. Second, you could seriously ask yourself whether you need a teacher anyway. Much of the advice in this book is about how to learn by putting yourself in charge rather than passively waiting for the teacher to tell you what to do.

Group C is a little imprecise since low marks and poor achievement are symptoms more than causes. Even so, it is useful to be clear as to whether getting poor results brings you to a halt or not. If it does then the cure lies in getting some good results quickly. And it is helpful to recognise that this is a problem which you control. You can cure poor performance.

Group D is all about what connections you see between the subject and your needs and interests. As some of the previous activities have shown, it is possible that you should not be studying your course at all. But assuming that your course is right for you, there are lots of ways of making a topic come alive for you. This will be explored in the section on 'How to generate motivation' in this chapter and in the whole of Chapter 3.

Broadly speaking, the problems above fall into three categories:

- learning problems;
- teaching problems;
- motivation problems.

Your most important step in dealing with problems which cause you to get stuck is to identify the type of problem you have. You should have reached this point by now.

Is it worth going on?

I hope the answer is 'yes'; certainly this section is not intended to put you off completing your course. What this section attempts is to show you a method of establishing what you do want to achieve and why.

Activity 2.5

Complete this activity using the 'tasks on which you get stuck' from Activity 2.4, but here you number them 11 to 20 rather than 1 to 10 – you will see why shortly. For each task, imagine that you had been able to complete it. Write down what short- or long-term benefit you would have gained from this.

In Activity 2.2 you had ten tasks that you like doing together with their rewards. You have just identified ten tasks on which you get stuck and their potential benefits. By comparing the two lists, you should be able to clarify which tasks you really wish to commit yourself to doing. This is your next activity.

Activity 2.6   Comparing tasks you like and tasks you do not like

This activity helps you to identify how important various tasks are to you by asking you to compare the benefits that each brings. To complete this activity use the extrinisic rewards of Activity 2.2 (numbering them 1 to 10) and the long-term benefits of Activity 2.5 (numbering them 11 to 20).

Work across each row of the table below, comparing each reward with each benefit. Ask yourself which is the most important to you. For example, if reward 5 is more important than benefit 13, put '5' in the cell where reward 5 and benefit 13 meet. Carry on until every cell in the table is filled.

Benefit

	11	12	13	14	15	16	17	18	19	20
1										
2										
3										
4										
5										
6										
7										
8										
9										
10										

Now count how many times you entered each reward and benefit and list them in the tables below:

Reward no	Entries		Benefit no	Entries
1			11	
2			12	
3			13	
4			14	

Finally, rank your results, starting with the reward or benefit with the highest number of entries in the two tables above. Remember that the highest score that any benefit or reward can have is ten and the lowest is zero.

Score(highest to lowest)	Benefit/reward number
10	
9	
8	
7	

Interpretation

You are exploring whether any of the ten things with which you get stuck are worth completing. To do this you are comparing the benefits that their completion would bring with the rewards of tasks that you like. So, how do your comparisons rate? Or, more pointedly, where do the scores for your benefits lie?

Any benefits which scored six or more are clearly important to you – they scored well even when compared with the rewards of the things that you like. The tasks that lead you to these benefits are well-worth continuing since, ultimately, you are going to value the benefits.

Finally, the benefits which scored zero, 1 or 2 hardly seem to be benefits at all (to you, at least) since you value them so little. Any task which yields such poor benefits seems a doubtful one for you to pursue.

Activity 2.7   The 'keep' and 'drop' lists

Ideally, Activity 2.6 should enable you to draw up a list of tasks which you would wish to continue, and a list of tasks which you now wish to drop. Since I asked you to select only ten easy and ten hard tasks, and since I asked you to make a deliberately wide choice, your lists will not necessarily cover everything that you want to sort out. If you would like to draw up a 'keep list' and a 'drop list', repeat the above activities as follows:

Activities 2.1 and 2.2 using the ten most important things that you like doing and find easy to do.

Activities 2.4 and 2.5 using the ten most important things that you find hard to do or get stuck with.

Your results should then enable you to decide which tasks clearly are important to you (the 'keep list') and which are not (the 'drop list').

2.4   How to generate motivation

So far I have talked of motivation as if it were a fixed thing and you have explored your own motivation in a similar way. In practice, there is much that you can do to generate your own motivation, or to get others to help you to do so. I shall look at five methods of increasing motivation:

- linking study to rewards which you control,
- making a 'public' commitment to completing certain stages of your study;
- breaking up the full task into smaller tasks;
- do something – anything – as a means of getting started;
- finding a small success.

Method 1   Linking study to rewards which you control

If you are on a long course leading to some remote reward such as passing an exam, I have already observed that this is not very helpful as a form of immediate motivation. No other form of motivation may be offered by your tutor, college or whoever. So you must provide the motivation yourself.

One very effective method is to reward yourself for completing small steps, e.g. for mastering one learning objective (see Chapter 1). What usually works is to choose some pleasurable activity that you would engage in even if you were not studying, and delay it until you have completed your task – e.g. you might like to watch television, dig the garden or play football. You then say to yourself, 'When I have completed . . ., I will let myself . . .'.

Activity 2.8   Rewards which work for you

Identify five rewards that you will use in future as motivations for your study.

Method 2   Making a public commitment

This is a very effective method. Instead of just completing your timetable and setting yourself tasks for the week, day or whatever, you tell someone close to you about your commitment and you enlist their help in keeping to your schedule. Your helper's task is to:

- know clearly what you have commited yourself to achieving and in how long;
- ask you from time to time about your progress;
- remind you of your commitment;
- assist you in rewarding yourself for successful completion.

All this may sound rather heavy-handed, suggesting that life will be one long nag. But, the very knowledge that you have made the commitment – that someone else will know if you abandon your task – is usually enough to ensure success. The helper rarely needs to intervene.

Activity 2.9   Choosing a helper

Identify someone who could help you to keep to your targets.

Method 3   Breaking up the task

You have met this already in Chapter 1 as part of the process of setting objectives. At this stage, I simply want to remind you of its role in increasing motivation. Many a task can seem so big that we are too daunted to make a start. Whether it is repairing the house or completing a course of study, the difficulty is the same. If you rigorously follow the method set out in Chapter 1 for preparing objectives, then you can overcome the problem. Once you have the separate objectives, you can stop thinking of your course as 'the course' and think of it as 'the objective that I have to master this week is . . .'.

Method 4   Do something – anything

You can use this method when you are having difficulty in making a start on study, particularly on making a start at something difficult or large (such as an essay or a project). The idea is to do anything – yes, absolutely anything – that is related to what you are trying to do. Try to keep it going for five to ten minutes. Then switch to the real task. All this may sound too simple to work, but it does for many people.

Method 5   Finding a small success

This final method is similar to 'Do something – anything' but is a more specific version. The idea is to re-trigger your interest through achieving something that makes you feel good. So you choose a task that is small –

but still significant – which you feel confident you can master. You then complete the task and acknowledge your success to yourself, perhaps by one of your rewards.

2.5 Feedback

Strictly this is just another way of increasing motivation, but it is so important that it merits its own section.

Imagine learning to play the piano if you were absolutely deaf and could not even feel the vibrations of the piano. You would be able to read the music, put your fingers on the keys and theoretically learn to play. But the essence of learning to play the piano is to adjust which keys you press, how hard you press them and for how long you press them. in response to what you hear. You hear that you play a chord too loud, and so you play it more softly next time. The noise of your playing provides feedback to aid your learning. Now if you were deaf, you would have no feedback. At best, someone else would have to tell you how to adjust your playing – but you would still depend on your helper to tell you whether you had got it right.

An extreme example, but one carefully chosen to highlight how difficult it is to learn unless you have feedback. This feedback serves two purposes. First, it helps you to adjust your learning. I will discuss this aspect more in Chapter 3. Second, it gives you a sense of achievement which then motivates you to keep going. Any attempt to learn without feedback is bound to be demotivating. Remember how you felt if your work was not marked at school?

Activity 2.10 How do you get feedback?

Write down a list of all the items that you have studied in the seven days ending yesterday. Then note down how either you have received feedback on them, or will receive feedback on them. If the answer is 'none' then write 'none'.

Activity 2.11 Increasing feedback

Quite possibly you could benefit from the additional motivation which would arise from more feedback. Think of some study items in the recent past on which you had little or no feedback. Try to think of how you could have obtained feedback on these.

I cannot know what feedback ideas you have generated, but here are some that other learners have used:

- exchanging work with a friend;
- forming a learners' self-help group;
- using textbooks designed for private study, i.e. ones which contain exercises and activities with detailed feedback.

⬡3⬡ Learning and feedback

3.1 Learning for what?

Education has often given the impression that all learning is of one kind: memorising information. Many teaching techniques reinforce this: lecturing, copying notes from the board, dictating notes and so on. In this chapter I want to take a more detailed look at:

- what we learn;
- how we learn (or should learn) different things;
- why we learn different things.

Activity 3.1   What you have learnt

This activity uses the same categories as Activity 1.3 in which you looked at things that you find easy and hard to learn. This time you are going to explore learning different categories of material within your course area and so find out how you ought to learn each one.

For each category below, write down two examples of the category that you have learnt on your current (or a recent) course.

Category	Examples
Facts	
Physical skills	
Concepts	
Rules	
Application	

If your course has encouraged you to think that all learning is simply remembering, then you may have found this activity quite hard. Do not worry. One function of this section is to help you to understand more about what you are learning and so to choose the most effective way to approach each topic. As a starting-point, you will look at the way that you learnt each of the items above.

Activity 3.2   How you have learnt

Using your examples from Activity 3.1, think back to the method by which you learnt the items. Your methods might have included: lectures, remembering by heart, discussion, trying examples etc. Write your methods down here:

Category	Learning methods used
Facts	
Physical skills	
Concepts	
Rules	
Application	

Now try answering the following questions about your methods:

1. How well do you match your learning method to the type of material to be learnt?
2. Do you tend to tackle different categories of learning by the same method?
3. Do you feel that you have not found effective methods for certain types of learning? Which types?

Before I move on to methods which might help with problems raised by your answers to these questions, I will look at one more aspect of learning – the question why?

3.2 Why?

Here I do not mean 'Why are you learning French, Maths or Engineering?' but 'What are you going to do with each item that you learn?'. Knowing this, can help you to learn it in a useful way. Here are some examples to illustrate my point:

Item to learn	Why?	Appropriate method
Telephone number	To make a call now.	'Hold' it in your memory, long enough to dial.
A formula	To repeat it in test.	Memorise thoroughly.
A formula	To solve problems with it.	Understand its structure, its components, when it can be used. Practise solving problems.
Spanish	For conversation.	Memorise structures. Memorise vocabulary. Practise structures with vocabulary.

Activity 3.3   Why?

Now it is your turn to look at why you are learning different items. Use your examples from Activity 3.1. Write down the use to which each item will be put.

I hope that by now you have a good feel for two aspects of your learning:

● you learn many different types of material;
● different items need different learning methods.

I shall finish this section with some general guidelines about how to learn different types of material. This list is not exhaustive and some of its methods may not work well for you. If you have found a better way, stick to it.

Learning facts

Since this is largely a matter of memorising, this will be covered in Chapter 5.

Physical skills

(e.g. driving, playing musical instruments and games)
The principles here are very easy – applying them can be very hard, as in the case of a musical instrument.

Any physical skill is made up of a number of steps. For example, consider a three-point-turn in a car. To do this, you need to be able to:

- choose a safe place to execute the turn;
- position the car at the kerb to start the turn;
- use your mirror;
- put the car into first gear;
- control the motion of the car through clutch control;
- use the hand brake;
- put the car into reverse gear.

The steps in learning to do a three-point-turn are:

- master each of the above skills separately;
- link the skills together, building up the sequence from the start;
- practise the whole sequence.

It sounds simple, but frequently people practise a whole skill when they have not first mastered its components. So, in summary, to learn a physical skill:

- Master each component skill by itself.
- Practise linking the skills together in the correct order – never practise in any other order.
- Practise the whole sequence.
- If you are not doing well, check:
  (a) is there a component skill that you need to practise more?
  (b) is there a link between two skills that you need to practise more?

Concepts

Concepts can be learnt by observation or from definitions. I shall look at concept learning by observation first.

Basically a concept is an idea which helps us to understand something complicated. For example, we see in colour. To be able to talk about and describe what we see, we need a way to describe different colours. So we have developed concepts such as 'blue', 'green', etc. Take the concept of 'red' as an example. A person understands the concept of red when that person correctly places objects into the two categories 'red' and 'not red'. Someone who does not understand the concept of red will make mistakes in allocating objects to the two groups. This is illustrated in Figures 3.1 and 3.2.

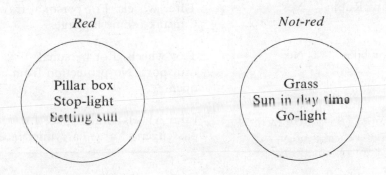

Figure 3.1 Decisions of a person who understands 'red'

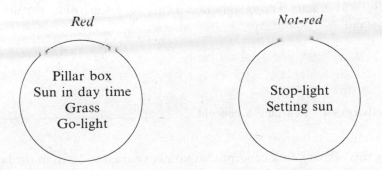

Figure 3.2 Decisions of a person who does not understand 'red'

To learn concepts by observation you need to:

- find a large number of examples on which to test the concept
- allocate them into two columns (see below)
- in the 'comments' column, record for yourself why the examples do or do not fit the concept.

Example on concept of 'motor car'
This is an interesting example since all of us are quite sure just what a car is. As you can see, it's not an easy thing to define.

Example	Fits? Yes/No	Comments
Ford Escort	Yes	Four wheels. For personal travel. Can take some luggage.
Reliant Robin	Yes	Three wheels. For personal travel. Can take some luggage.
Motor bike	No	Two wheels. For personal transport. No protection from open.
Lorry	No	Four wheels. Some space for passengers. Large carrying space.

This is a good example of how difficult it can be to understand some concepts. If I were to try adding a motor-bike with sidecar and an open sports car to the list, it would become even harder to decide just what makes a car a car. Trying this task helps to reveal what we do not understand.

Activity 3.4   Learning a concept

Try this activity on a concept that you have tried to learn in the last few weeks, but that have found that you do not fully understand yet.

What is the concept?

Describe the broad characteristics of things that fit the concept.

Describe the broad characteristics of things that do not fit the concept.

Now try to find five examples that fit the concept and five that do not, entering them in the table below.

Example	Fits? Yes/No	Comments
1.		
2.		
3.		
4.		
5.		
6.		
7.		
8.		
9.		
10.		

Reflect on the above and try to determine whether you now understand the concept better.

Rules and defined concepts

Some concepts are learnt from definitions rather than experience or observation, e.g. 'live mains electricity connections are dangerous to touch' is a rule which cannot sensibly be learnt by experience. We all have to learn it from the written or spoken statement. How should such rules be learnt?

First, you should note that it is not enough to be able to repeat the words 'live mains electricity connections are dangerous to touch'. We would only be satisfied that someone understood the rule if they could demonstrate what was and what was not safe to touch.

To learn (including to understand) rules you should:

- Check that you understand each concept that makes up the rule. In the above example, the rule uses the concepts of 'mains electricity', 'connections', 'dangerous' and 'touch'. A person who failed to understand even one of these concepts could not understand the rule.
- Explore how each concept is linked to the next in the definition.
- Think of examples of where the rule applies and where it does not.

Activity 3.5   Learning a rule

Using the rule 'cars should drive on the left-hand side of the street in the UK':

- identify the concepts which are used in this rule;
- ask yourself how the concepts link together;
- list five examples where the rule applies and where it does not.

This activity reveals an important point about rule-learning: you often find that the rule is a bit vague. In your notes, you can record for yourself extensions which help to make the rule clearer. For example, the rule does not make it clear what is to happen in one-way streets.

Problem-solving

If someone offers to help you to learn to solve problems by showing you the solutions, say, 'No thank you'. You cannot learn to solve problems by observation or by reading books of 'solved problems' (these books do have a use which I will explain in a later chapter).

Basically, problem-solving involves using a set of rules to reach a solution to something. Formal problem-solving occurs most in mathematics and the sciences but it occurs on a lesser scale in many subjects. Your capacity to solve problems depends on how well you can:

- identify all the rules that might apply to the problem;
- understand those rules thoroughly;
- identify all the features of the problem;
- form hypotheses about the problem.

That is all a bit tough in theory but much clearer when you apply it to something that you have tried to learn. The next activity does this.

Activity 3.6   Problem-solving

Think back over your last few weeks of study and try to identify at least three problems which you tried to solve but could not. They need to be examples where you have subsequently been shown the solution. For each problem, ask yourself which of the four solution stages was the cause of your problem:

Problem	Causes of difficulty			
	Identifying rules	Understanding rules	Features of problem	Forming hypotheses
1				
2				
3				

This should begin to identify where you need to put most effort to improve your problem-solving.

3.3   To understand or not to understand?

Some things are clearly more difficult to remember than others. For example, it is difficult to remember the number of days in each month, or the names of the notes in the treble clef. To help us remember this sort of information we often convert it into some other form. e.g. for the months we remember the rhyme:

> Thirty days hath September,
> April, June and dark November.
> All the rest have thirty-one
> Saving February alone
> Which has twenty-eight days clear
> And twenty-nine in each leap year.

For the treble clef, we remember 'FACE' for the spaces and 'Every Good Boy Deserves Favour' for the lines.

What these familiar examples illustrate is that it is easier to remember something which has meaning or pattern than something which has no pattern and that we do not understand.

Activity 3.7   Learning without understanding

Try to learn the following four line poem by heart. Time how long you take over it – or how long before you give up!

> boe opx uifsf dbnf apui njtu boe topx,
> boe ju hsfx xpoespvt dpme:
> boe jdf, nbtu-ijhi, dbnf gmpbujoh cz,
> bt hsffo bt fnfsbne.

How could it take so long to learn 24 words or 95 letters? Does it always take this long? Here is another poem of exactly the same length. See how long it takes you to learn this one.

> And now there came both mist and snow,
> And it grew wondrous cold:
> And ice, mast-high, came floating by,
> As green as emerald.

(Verse 13 of 'The Rime of the Ancient Mariner', by Samuel Taylor Coleridge; *Oxford Book of English Verse*, 1968)

You will certainly have found the second poem easier to learn than the first. Yet the first poem is only the second one with each letter replaced by the next one in the alphabet. By changing the letters, I have destroyed the pattern and the meaning, creating a near-impossible learning task.

The example above is artificial but every day thousands of students put themselves through the same impossible learning tasks. They stare at notes on topics which they have not understood, hoping vainly to memorise them.

Activity 3.8   Analysing what you remember

Write down five specific things (e.g. French verbs) which you find easy to remember and five which you do not.

Now take your lists and examine the extent to which you understand the ten topics. If you are not sure whether you understand a topic, ask yourself whether you can use it, whether you can apply it to something. If you can, then you probably understand it.

I hope that you have found some connection between what you understand and can use on the one hand and what you find easy to remember on the other. All this illustrates the importance of understanding. There is a golden rule here:

NEVER ATTEMPT TO MEMORISE WHAT YOU DO NOT UNDERSTAND.

In the next section, I will show you how you can make sure that you do understand material.

3.4 Making it meaningful

A leading educational psychologist, David Ausubel, has introduced the idea of meaningful learning to education. This section attempts to show how you can use this idea to help you with your learning.

___ Activity 3.9 Exploring some meaningful items _____

Think of two things which you have recently learnt that were fairly tough to learn, but which you now feel you understand quite well. For each item, answer the following questions.

Question	Item 1	Item 2
In what way does the item make sense?		
Which parts of your previous knowledge were essential to learning this item?		
What active steps did you take to learn this item?		

I will look at each of these questions in turn.

Making sense

Almost certainly what you have learnt makes sense in some way or other. There are dozens of ways in which we can say something makes sense, e.g.

- it fits the facts;
- it fits our experience;
- it helps to explain previously inexplicable phenomena;
- the material is internally coherent – it does not contradict itself;
- it works when we use it, e.g. it helps us solve problems, build bridges, cure illness.

On the other hand, we would suspect a piece of learning that did not make sense, if it had the opposite characteristics:

- it does not fit the facts;
- it does not fit our experience;
- it does not help explain any phenomenon;
- it contradicts itself;
- it does not work when we apply it.

Normally human beings only feel comfortable with learning that makes sense. Our brains seem to need meaningfulness before they will accept new information.

Previous knowledge

It is not enough for something to make sense for us to be able to learn it. Imagine that you are shown how to solve simultaneous equations such as:

$$2x + 3y = 7$$
$$x + 2y = 4$$

You would be totally lost if you did not know:

- elementary arithmetic;
- what 'x' and 'y' mean;
- what '$2x$' means;
- what an equation is;
- how to manipulate equations.

So even an apparently simple piece of learning is based on a large number of items of prior learning.

If you find it hard to understand something, ask yourself 'Is the problem that I do not understand what comes before this?'

Taking active steps to relate it to what you know
You have met the first two requirements for meaningful learning: the material itself must make sense and you must have the necessary prior knowledge. But that is still not enough for the learning to happen. You have to want the learning to happen and become actively involved in it. The next section explores this in more depth.

3.5 Active learning

If you have been working your way through this book from the beginning, you will have a good idea of what I mean by active learning. You should have done far more writing, thinking, evaluating, etc., than pure reading of my text. But there is still more to active learning, and this section will explore some of the methods available.

Activity 3.10   What does activity mean to you?

Look back over your last two weeks of learning and consider which of the following active learning methods you used. Rate your usage on the scale 'Never' to 'Very often'.

Method	Rating				
	Never	Hardly	Some times	Quite often	Very often
Asking questions					
Rewriting in your own words					
Summarising					
Relating to previous knowledge					
Discussing with someone else					
Solving problems					
Applying the knowledge					

You do not need to feel that you have to have ticked 'Very often' for everything – not all methods are equally useful for all topics. However, if you do not have many 'Quite often' or 'Frequently', perhaps you need to try some of these methods more. A look at the way that they work might encourage you.

Quite often we talk as if our brains were empty pots waiting to be filled. 'I just can't get it into my head' and 'My head's too full of other things' both illustrate this view. More recently, people have begun to compare their memories to those of electronic digital computers, despite the fact that our brains are totally different from computers. Since the computer model is so dominant today, it is useful to look at the three ways in which we are radically different from a computer.

A computer stores each item of information in a fixed place in its memory. So it could store the statement 'The Battle of Hastings took place in 1066' in a definite place (or, more precisely, in 41 places, one for each letter and space). Second, the computer stores exactly that information – no more, no less. Third, the computer cannot connect that information with anything else in its memory. You could ask the computer to store the statements 'There is no such place as Hastings' and '1066 never existed', and it would.

Clearly our brains work very differently. When you try to learn the fact 'The Battle of Hastings took place in 1066', four things happen:

- You check that it makes sense.
- You check your memory for related knowledge (e.g. what else do you know about Hastings, battles, or 1066?).
- You create your own version of the statement 'The Battle of Hastings took place in 1066'. This might include mental pictures of the battle or your feelings about it.
- You 'store' this information in lots of different parts of your brain.

We cannot picture how this all looks, but it seems that the brain spreads information around and links each new item to what is already there. This is illustrated in a very crude sense in Figure 3.3.

The attempt to learn new information triggers new links between the new information and what we already know. Whilst we understand very little about this, we do know:

- the more active your learning, the more easily the links are made;
- the more links you make, the more easily that item is recalled;
- the more links you make, the longer the item is remembered.

Possibly in a crude way, we can say that the more links you make, the better you understand something. All the 'active learning' methods discussed in this section and elsewhere in this book are ways of building those links in your brain.

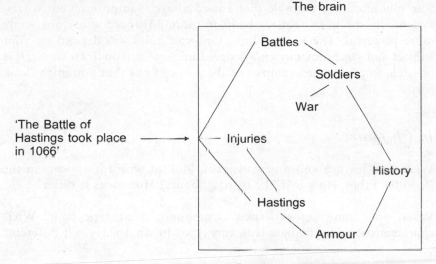

Figure 3.3 Storing a fact in our brains

3.6 Relating material to previous knowledge

Although this method was mentioned in the last section, it is sufficiently important to have a section of its own.

You have seen how new knowledge forms links with existing knowledge and I used the word 'crude' about this model of the way that we learn. One key idea that Figure 3.3 cannot demonstrate is that each piece of new information has the potential to modify our previous learning. Here is a simple example.

Children learn multiplication tables by rote – that is, using pure memory without understanding. At that stage there is no connection between $3 \times 5 = 15$ and $5 \times 3 = 15$. Each has to be learnt as a separate fact. Later, children learn that multiplication is commutative, i.e. that $a \times b = b \times a$ always. This new knowledge changes the way that a child sees the multiplication tables – the tables automatically shrink to half their size for a start.

Activity 3.11   Relating material to previous knowledge

For this activity, use a selection of the same items that you used in Activity 3.10. For each item, consider in what ways you linked the item to previous knowledge, and in what further ways you could have done so.

Do you see how making more links would help you learn more easily?

The multiplication example that I used above is important but trivial. Potentially the links that we build in more advanced study are vastly more powerful. The kind of links that you build will depend on your subject and your previous knowledge. Links are personal. However, it is possible to give some examples of the sort of links that you might look for:

In Chemistry

When you learn about a new element, look at where it appears in the Periodic Table. How is it like its neighbours? How does it differ?

When you come across a new compound, what type is it? What characteristics does it share with this type? In what ways is it different?

Learning a foreign language

Vocabulary: when you come across a new word, does it have links with a word in English, e.g. in French 'la main – manual – hand' can help you link 'main' with 'hand'.

Learning maths

When you learn a new formula, see if it is related to other formulae that you know. How is it different?

Learning study skills

When you have a problem, ask yourself 'Have I had this problem before?' 'Can I learn from what I did last time?' When you hear of a new study hint (as in this book), try it out. Does it work for you? When? When not?

3.7 Knowing when you are right

How do you know when you have understood something correctly, got the right answer, or made a good job of something? One way is to leave the judgement to others. 'I don't know if it's any good. I'll wait and see what mark I get.' Often the test and marking systems in education encourage this attitude with the result that learners do not feel responsible for their own work. This is not the best way to learn. Learning is faster, easier, more confident if you take charge of 'knowing when you are right'. As you will see, this does not mean that you never ask for the opinions or judgements of others but it does mean that you control the process of checking your own understanding.

Activity 3.12 Have you been checking?

Look back over five topics that you have learnt recently, choosing as wide a range as possible. In each case, try to identify how you checked your understanding or mastery of the topic.

Now consider whether the method that you used for checking was fully effective. How sure are you that you really know how well you mastered the topic?

Assuming that your checking methods were not the best that you could possibly have used, try now to think of some more effective methods that you could have used.

By now you have probably exhausted the checking methods with which you are familiar so now I will suggest a range that may include some new ideas for you. You may not be surprised to find that, yet again, the category of what you are learning or doing determines how you can check your progress. To recap, the categories used in this book are:

- facts;
- physical skills;
- concepts;
- rules;
- application.

Facts

These are the easiest to check. You simply need to reproduce the fact, e.g. by:

- writing them down – then comparing them with your notes, etc.;
- verbally responding to questions from a friend who checks with your notes at the same time.

Physical skills

There are two aspects to check: what you do and what the result is.
  To check what you do:

- Form a clear list of the steps or components of the skills, e.g. the leg movement of the crawl.
- Watch and analyse others performing the same skill, picking out the steps and forming a clear mental image of them.
- As you practise the skill, consciously observe yourself going through each step, comparing it with the correct action.

To check the result is much easier than checking the action. Write down which results show you are doing well and which results show you are doing badly. Compare these with your own performance.

Concepts

Concepts can only be tested through application. It is no use just checking that you can recall your notes. For example, consider the concept of a rectangle. You might have notes which say 'a rectangle is a parallelogram with internal angles of 90 degrees'. Being able to repeat or recall this does not show an understanding of 'rectangle'. To show that you understand it you might:

- draw examples of rectangles;
- draw examples of figures which are not rectangles and state why;
- from a collection of figures, state which are rectangles.

In general, to check your understanding of a concept you need to:

- produce examples of the concept;
- produce examples of what is not the concept;
- identify correct and incorrect applications of the concept.

Rules

As with concepts, you must avoid the assumption that memorising a rule is the same as understanding it. Consider the rule 'when approaching a roundabout, vehicles should give way to traffic from the right'. Would you trust your life to someone who could state the rule but had never driven on the road? Proof of understanding is in the correct application of the rule. In this example, we might be satisfied that someone understood the rule if:

- on ten approaches to a variety of roundabouts, the rule was correctly interpreted
- given ten examples of incorrect application, the errors were all correctly identified.

In general, when you wish to check your understanding of rules check that you can:

- correctly identify situations to which the rule does and does not apply
- use the rule in practice to achieve its stated purpose, e.g. to solve a problem
- identify errors in the incorrect application of the rule.

Application

Application is more difficult to check than the basic parts of learning, but there are some things which you can do to see if you are probably right.

First, check that you have analysed all the parts of the problem or system correctly. Examples of analysis are:

- Describing the components of a car engine and how they fit together.
- Describing the circulation of the blood and the correct relationship of the heart, veins, arteries, lungs etc.

So, analysis is about:

- parts;
- how parts fit together.

To check your capacity to analyse what you are studying, you should:

- draw concept maps (see Chapter 4, Section 4.4) for (a) your whole subject and (b) more detailed sections of it;
- organise as much of what you learn into lists, tables and diagrams that show how each topic, rule, concept, etc., relates to what you are learning;
- always check that you can explain the connection between what you are learning now and what you already know.

Second, you have to use the parts (or a selection of them) in your application. Examples of application are:

- writing an essay that substantiates a point of view;
- designing a new machine or electrical circuit;
- composing a piece of music;
- producing a plan or a set of recommendations for action to solve a problem.

All this is very difficult to check because there are no 'right' answers when you are creating something new. But you can check that what you have produced:

- takes account of all the facts (and not just those in your favour);
- works in practice (e.g. that it solves the problem).

Problem-solving

In this discussion I shall only consider the formal type of problem-solving that you find in education, e.g. problems like 'Solve $5x + 2 = 7$' rather than problems like 'How can we end world hunger?'

Many such problems are of the type 'Show that . . .', 'Prove that . . .', in which case it is generally fairly simple to check whether you are right. Where the problem is more like 'Find . . .', you have to delve deeper to check your work. You can check:

- Is the answer sensible? (An answer 'Height of man = 3cm' does seem less than plausible.)
- Does the answer fit the original data?
- Would any other answer fit just as well? If so, how can you decide which is more likely to be right?
- What follows from the answer? Is that sensible, or does the answer's consequences make the answer look suspect?

3.8   Learning from mistakes

The human brain is designed to learn from mistakes – or, more correctly, from detecting deviations from our intended performance. Try to remember what it was like learning to ride a bicycle. First you lean too much to the left. A falling sensation tells you that you are not upright. So you lean to the right, but again too far. Once again you are aware of your leaning position and so you correct the lean.

There is no way anyone could simply sit on a bike and ride it perfectly first time. Equally, there is no way that anyone could learn to ride a bicycle without the feedback which our brains give us as to the mistakes we are making.

This is, of course, an example of unconscious use of feedback from our errors. It all happens too quickly for us to be able to analyse it. Still, the principle can be applied at the conscious level as well. We can learn to learn from our mistakes.

Activity 3.13   Spotting learning opportunities

Every mistake is a learning opportunity. Try to identify five mistakes which you have made recently in your study, and what action you took.

Now consider what you could have done in a more positive sense to learn from those mistakes.

Spotting your mistakes

Who finds your mistakes? Do you wait until a tutor has marked your work or do you find mistakes for yourself? There is a lot of evidence to show that students do not see their mistakes as a valuable source of learning. Many complete their work, hand it in, wait for its return, look at the mark and . . . well, that is usually it. In this way they miss one of the most powerful learning devices there is: analysing our mistakes.

Consider some typical mistakes and how we can learn from them.

- In mathematics, students will often use the wrong formula to attempt a solution. This shows the need to spend more time understanding when a formula should be used. Lots of practice identifying when a formula can and cannot be used would help.
- In learning a foreign language, repeatedly making the same grammatical error – perhaps not making nouns and adjectives agree in French. The cure might be to (a) revise the rules then (b) work through several pages of French text looking for examples of the rules, checking that you understand each case, then (c) practise on a piece of writing of your own.
- In physics, confusing two similar concepts such as weight and mass. To overcome this, you might (a) revise the explanations and definitions of the two concepts, then (b) list as many examples of each as you can imagine, writing an explanation against each as to why it is 'weight' or 'mass'.

Time spent on activities of this type is highly productive. You not only overcome your mistakes but reinforce your understanding of the basics of your subject in the process.

Activity 3.14   Analysis over a long period

This is potentially a very large activity. Skip it on a first reading of this book but try it when you can spare several hours. One very good time to try it is at the start of a block of revision. It will direct your revision to where it is most needed.

Take all your work for a given period, e.g. a term or a course. Go through it, listing all the mistakes you made, trying to group similar mistakes together. Then work through each grouping of mistakes to analyse why you made them and what action you need to take to overcome them.

4 Information: finding and using it

4.1 Information for what?

We are living in possibly the first century to suffer from having far too much information. Most of us are overloaded with paper, radio, television, meetings and so on. One reaction is to attempt to absorb it all. Another is to panic. The first can never be achieved – information is generated faster than we can ever process it. The second gets us nowhere. Our only hope of coping is to be highly selective about what information we need and, to achieve that, we need to know why we need the information.

Activity 4.1   Being selective

Imagine that you need to carry out the four tasks below. What information would you need? What information should you ignore?

Task	Need	Ignore
Baking a cake		
Planning a motorway journey		
Writing a topic on India		
Choosing someone to read the news		

57

Your lists and mine may vary a bit – particularly when it comes to what to ignore, but I hope you at least do not disagree with the following.

Task	Need	Ignore
Baking a cake	Ingredients Quantities How to mix/process Cooking times	Author's digression on where he/she found the recipe
Planning a motorway journey	Motorway numbers Junction numbers to enter/leave	Towns passed Counties passed through
Writing a topic on India	Impossible to decide on this one. The topic is too wide to give any criteria for what should be included or excluded	
Choosing someone to read the news	Voice Manner Appearance	Sex Race Height Weight

Activity 4.2   Selecting for a study task

You can complete this activity for any typical study task which you have recently attempted or are currently working on. For the task, identify the criteria which will determine the information that you should use.

● list some typical items of information that you will use.
● list some examples of information that you will not use.

Almost certainly you have completed pieces of work in the past where you have used too much information: the essay that needed a few pieces of evidence to support an argument but which you packed with pages of detail; the question that asked you to list two examples but where you wrote three paragraphs. Most formal educational tasks are designed to be completed using very little information. The skill being tested is, partly, your capacity to select the appropriate information and use it intelligently. Here are some danger signs which should suggest you are using too much information:

- You have given more than three examples.
- You are putting down everything that you know on the topic.
- You are writing quickly but will still find it difficult to complete the task in the allotted time.
- You have written twice as much as anyone else.
- It will take your tutor a very long time to mark what you have written.

All the time, the key principle is 'be selective'. How you select depends on your purpose. There are lots of methods available as the following activity illustrates.

Activity 4.3   Information selection methods

Listed below are a variety of approaches to selecting information to put into a piece of your work. Against each one, make a note of when each method might be useful to you.

Method	*Possible use*
1. Taking a brief quotation from a longer piece	
2. Summary of main points, dropping the detail	
3. Selecting a few examples	
4. Drawing a summary diagram	
5. Selecting a complete chunk, e.g. a whole diagram	

When these methods might be useful to you is for you to decide, but here are some of my ideas.

Quotations
These are useful when you want to support an argument of your own, e.g. in an essay, but you have very little space for additional material.

Summary of main points
This is a useful approach if you want to keep the information in a fairly extended form to work on later. (But you will see later on that this is not the best form in which to make notes for later revision.)

Selected examples
Often you do not need all an author's argument because you already have many other sources of material. In that case you would just select the few examples where that author had something new or special to say.

Diagrammatic summary
Words soon confuse. They give us too much information and not in a digestible form. A diagrammatic summary of a book, a chapter, a theory, etc., can be a very powerful way of both understanding and remembering it. For example, drawing a time-chart or a family tree are both powerful aids to understanding.

Picking out odd pieces
Be selective. If the only new (or, to you, relevant) item that an author has to offer is one diagram, one table or one paragraph, then take it. Ignore the rest.

4.2   Sources of information

Activity 4.4   Which sources do you use?

Look back over the last four weeks of your study and record the sources of information which you used, together with their frequency.

Source	Frequency
e.g. Lecture notes	20 hours

You may be making the best of all the sources of information available to you, or there may be some that you have not thought of trying. Here is a possible list to consider:

- lecture notes
- textbooks
- revision aids (often far better written than textbooks)
- reference books
- radio and television
- newspapers (many now have regular features on computers, the environment, the law, etc.)
- magazines and journals (e.g. *The Economist*, *The New Scientist* and many subject-specific magazines)
- family
- friends
- specialist societies (often with their own magazine and their own reference libraries)
- national organisations
- museums and art galleries
- newspaper archives (ask at your reference library)
- on-line databases (ask at your reference library).

And so it goes on and on. Intimidated? You should be. There is far too much for any one of us to tackle without a very clear strategy. As you saw in the section on 'Information for what?', you have to be very selective. So, before approaching any information source – even a book – you need to have clear answers to the questions:

- What am I looking for?
- What will I reject/skip?
- How much information do I need?

But why do it all alone? If you are on a course with other students, you could share the information sifting and gathering. One could check '*The Times*', another '*The Economist*', another the local museum . . . Yes, some tutors do still frown on cooperative activity but I prefer cooperation to competition.

___ **Activity 4.5   Sources you plan to use** _____

Take a look forward to your study over the next few weeks. What five key information sources will you use for what purposes?

4.3 Reading methods

You may well ask whether there is more than one method of reading. Don't we just start at the top left-hand corner of the page and work across the lines from left to right? You may think that that is how you always read, but almost certainly that is not the case. How do you read when faced with a list of names, and you only want to find your own? How do you 'read' a newspaper – presumably not systematically from the top left-hand corner of page one to the bottom right-hand corner of the last page. I can be fairly certain therefore that you have several reading methods, selecting the appropriate one more or less automatically. Here I am going to say a little more about each so that you can select them more consciously and, possibly, to even better effect.

There are five types of reading – scanning, skimming, light reading, word-by-word reading and reading to study.

Scanning

This is how you search for your name in a list. You know what you want and pass your eyes over everything else. In some sense you clearly 'see' what you ignore because you notice enough to note that it is not what you want. However, after finding your name, you can recall nothing of what you have passed over.

Skimming

With skimming you again pass very quickly over a piece of text but not to find anything in particular. You skim 'to see what is there'. It gives you a general overview of an article, a chapter, or whatever. In skimming you try to note the rough content through headings, figure-titles, opening sentences of paragraphs, etc.

Skimming has two main uses. First, to decide whether the text is of any use to you. A skim may reveal that the material is irrelevant for your purposes. Second, as a warm-up before a more detailed study of the text.

Light reading

Most leisure reading is light reading. We read every work at a pace with which we feel comfortable. We usually make sure that we understand it all, but particularly boring, difficult or irrelevant passages will be skipped. We make no special effort to study or absorb the material.

On the whole, light reading is not of much value in study. Study-reading always requires either more or less detailed attention.

Word-by-word reading

Some material has to be read in very great detail for it to be understood at all. Examples are:

Type	Example
Foreign languages	'Longtemps, je me suis couché de bonne heure.' (The famous opening of Proust's 'Du Côte de Chez Swann')
Formulae	$x = \dfrac{-b \pm \sqrt{(b^2 - 4ac)}}{2a}$ (The formula for solving quadratic equations)
Unusual/complex words	Electroencephalography (More familiar as ECG)

In each of these cases we cannot read over the material at 100 to 200 words per minute (a typical light-reading speed). Indeed with maths or a foreign language, we might spend 20 to 50 minutes over a few lines of text.

Reading to study

The fifth and final method is one for the detailed study of something reasonably extensive such as a chapter of a book. The aim is to understand the material in depth. There are many ways to approach 'reading for study'. One is SQ3R which stands for:

• survey	S	⎫	The initial
• question	Q	⎪	letters of
• read	R	⎬	the five words
• recall	R	⎪	give the method
• review.	R	⎭	its name.

The method is simple but thorough. You just work through the five steps described above as follows.

Survey

Skim through the chapter to get an idea of what is in it. Make a note of the key items included.

Question

Write down a list of questions that you hope to be able to answer as a result of reading the chapter.

Read

Read the chapter slowly and carefully.

Recall

Close the book. Then from memory write down the main points that were made in the chapter. If very specific pieces of information (e.g. special vocabulary, formulae or diagrams) are of special importance, try to write them down from memory too.

Review

Go back to your questions from the 'Question' stage and see how well your 'Recall' stage has answered them. Fill in any gaps by further reading and note-taking.

Activity 4.6   Choosing reading methods

Think about the types of study and reading that you do. Try to identify tasks which could make use of the five reading methods.

Reading method	When you could use it
Scanning	
Skimming	
Light reading	
Word by word	
SQ3R	

4.4 Keeping information

In the first three chapters of this book I have said a lot about how personal memory and understanding are. Linking what you are trying to learn to what you already know is essential to learning. In this chapter you have already seen the importance of selecting information according to why you need it. It should therefore come as no surprise to you to know that how you keep information – your notes – is also very personal.

Activity 4.7 Why notes?

For many courses, it is now possible to buy excellent revision notes. Can you think of any reasons why such pre-prepared notes are not a total replacement for your own notes?

Reasons for keeping personal notes

There are many reasons for also keeping your own notes. The most important are:

- the process of making notes aids learning;
- your own notes follow a format which reflects how you think;
- in your own notes, you can build links to your previous knowledge;
- you can create your own memory aids – these are more powerful for you than other people's aids;
- your own notes can concentrate on those things which you find most difficult.

Most students are used to keeping notes which are a reasonable summary of what has been said in a lecture. Such notes often extend to hundreds of pages of closely-packed writing. They are near to useless because they contradict all that you have learnt so far in this book about learning. So how should you keep notes? First, some general principles, and then some methods that build on these.

General principles for good notes
Notes are there to:

- help you understand difficult concepts;
- help you recall factual information;
- link what you are learning to previous knowledge;
- highlight, dramatise and bring alive your study.

If notes are to achieve this they should:

- link new material to previous knowledge;
- give pattern to what you are learning;
- give structure to what you are learning;
- make things stand out;
- break down long or complex material into lots of small chunks.

There are many ways in which you can achieve this. No one way of making notes is best. What is 'best' is that you should try lots of methods so that you feel confident that you know which work for you.

Concept maps

A concept map is a way of showing the structure behind a topic or subject. It shows relationships between one item and another and so can be used to show links between what you are learning and your previous knowledge. For example, Figure 4.1 is a concept map for this book.

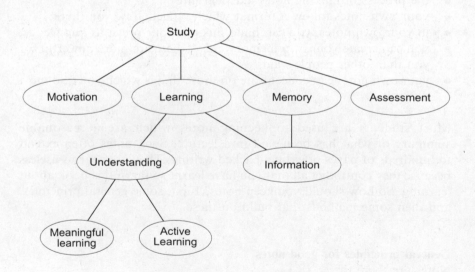

Figure 4.1   A concept map

The lines show the most important links between the topics – if I were to put all the minor links in, the diagram would be a confused mess.

___ **Activity 4.8   Making a concept map** ___ _____

Draw a concept map for your course, or for a major part of it.

Of course, you can take any one bubble from a concept map and develop it into a more detailed map by itself. You might do this for each part of your course.

Nuclear notes

Nuclear notes – also called spider diagrams – are a useful way of showing connections between lots of different items. They are similar to concept maps but are used for one topic only rather than a range of topics. For example, Figure 4.2 shows nuclear notes for this section on note-taking.

To create nuclear notes, you place the topic in a bubble at the centre of your page. (Hence the name 'nuclear' since the nucleus of something is at its centre.) Then for each major point (in Figure 4.2, 'Why keep notes?', 'General principles' and 'Special methods'), you draw a line out from the nucleus, labelling it with what it represents. Then, for each major line you draw branches off it for sub-points. If space permits and you have suitably neat handwriting, you may even wish to subdivide the sub-points. The limit of sub-division is up to you.

___ **Activity 4.9   Making nuclear notes** ___ _____

Practise making one set of nuclear notes for a topic on which you already have more conventional notes.

Other notes

Most other notes are a variant on the prose-style of lecture notes, but the method needs lots of effort to make it effective. Here are some important points to keep in mind:

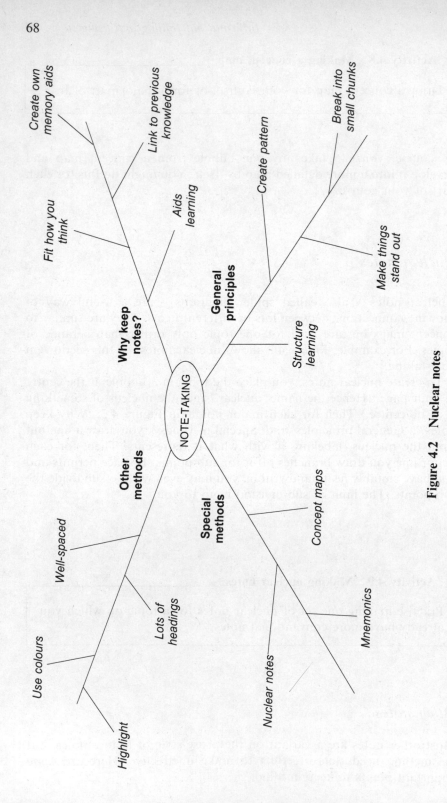

Figure 4.2 Nuclear notes

- keep your notes well-spaced;
- use lots of headings;
- use several colours;
- highlight differences (differences are easier to remember than similarities);
- devise lots of mnemonics;
- use lots of diagrams;
- add plenty of examples – especially memorable ones. Exaggeration and humour help.

Activity 4.10   Making notes memorable

Take three or four pages of your existing notes and prepare new notes using the above principles. Assume that you will use twice as much paper, but fewer words. Before you start writing, jot down a few ideas for:

- structure
- headings
- diagrams
- mnemonics
- wild, memorable, examples.

4.5   Processing information

You have already met the idea of processing information in the work that you have done on note-taking. The information which we receive is rarely in the best form for our purposes. Information-processing is what we do to it to put it in a form that suits us.

There are various reasons why what you receive may not suit you. These include:

- too much detail
- some items irrelevant
- ideas jumbled about
- connections not shown
- no indication of the relative importance of items.

Your purpose in processing the information will be to produce something which does one or more of the following:

- shows the required level of detail;
- includes only what matters to you;
- is clearly and logically set out;
- ideas are properly connected up;
- the most important items are highlighted.

The ideal is to meet all these requirements simultaneously.

It may be obvious to you by now that standard lecture notes are rarely in a form that anyone can use. The information is too dense, lacks impact and is poor at showing relationships. To emphasise this point, consider some 'classic' pieces of good information presentation.

Mnemonics

Unless you are a first-aider, you may feel hazy about what to do and in what order when you find someone who is clearly in a serious state after an accident or a heart attack. Just remember 'ABC':

Airway
Breathing
Circulation.

A powerful mnemonic. It tells you what to check and in which order.

Word diagrams

Most of us have heard of the carbon cycle or the periodic table. Both are word diagrams that provide easy understanding and assimilation of a mass of scientific material. For example, Figure 4.3 shows the carbon cycle from which all of us can get some measure of understanding. Imagine trying to understand a prose description of the same thing!

Pictorial diagrams

Imagine studying geography without maps or science without diagrams. Something as simple as a map of Africa (Figure 4.4) contains thousands of items of information – even the information to draw the coastline would be more than anyone could make sense of in anything but pictorial form. In a diagram we can all understand and remember it.

71

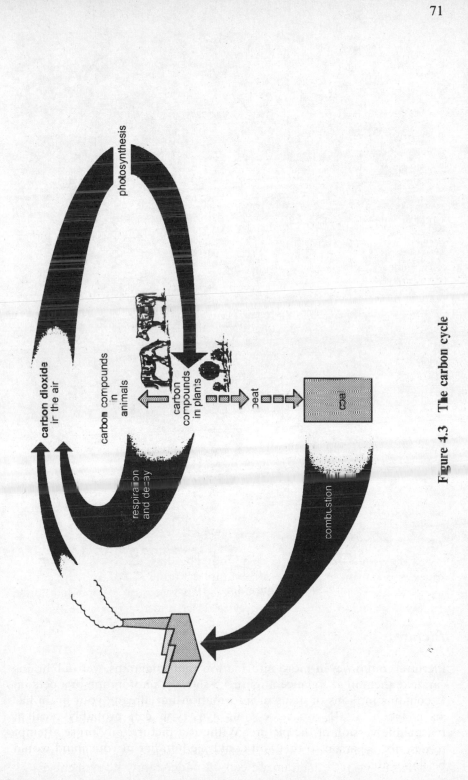

Figure 4.3 The carbon cycle

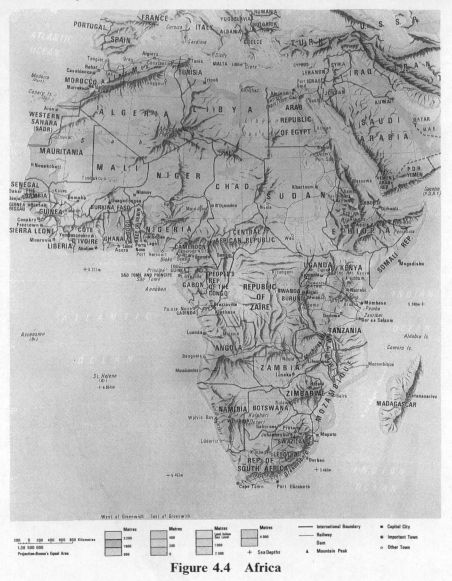

Figure 4.4   Africa

Pictures

Pictures contain even more information than diagrams, yet our brains can take them in at a glance. Figure 4.5 shows a photograph of a person. It contains millions of items of information but already your brain has an image of it. If you close your eyes, you can probably recall a reasonable version of the picture. Without a picture, any prose attempt to describe a person so that you could see him/her in your mind would be impossible.

Figure 4.5   A human face

So what does all this tell you? First, it tells you something about how to organise information for your learning. Second, it tells you something about presenting information to others.

Information for learning

You can see that you will learn more, more quickly and more effectively when your notes:

Maximise the use of	*Minimise the use of*
Pictures	Prose
Diagrams	Descriptions
Word diagrams	
Graphs	
Mnemonics	

Information for presentation

Exactly the same applies when you are presenting information to others. Whether informally, such as telling someone how to reach your home (draw a map), or formally, as in an exam, the same principles apply. Pictures, diagrams, charts, etc., get more information over, more meaningfully and more quickly.

Activity 4.11   Processing your notes

Take ten to twenty pages of your notes. Using several coloured pens, mark with your first colour those sections of your notes that could be changed to mnemonics; use another colour for sections that could be changed to word diagrams, and so on. If you are still left at the end with large chunks with no colour against them, have another go. At least 80 per cent of most notes can be converted in this way.

4.6   Internalising information

I have emphasised how personal learning is. What and how we learn depends on our motivations, on what we already know and on the learning methods which work for us. In the activities on notetaking and information-gathering which you have already done, you have been individualising the material on which you have been working. In this section, I will introduce some more specific techniques for making information personal to you – internalising it.

First, a reminder of the aim of internalising information. We do it because we remember better and understand better, knowledge which:

- is in a form which we have created;
- is in a form that fits our personal learning preferences;
- links to what we already know.

There are lots of ways of achieving this – you may well have invented a few of your own – but here are some suggestions:

- Rewrite all the information in your own words.
- For each point made in the information, write down an example from your own experience.
- Reorganise the information into pictures, charts, etc. of your own design.
- For each topic write down how it connects with what you already know. Does it support, illustrate or contradict your previous knowledge?
- For each topic, write down what you feel about it. Is it believable, useful, sensible?
- Imagine that you had to explain a topic to someone who knew nothing about it. Write down how you would present it to them.

Here are some activities to help you to practise some of these methods.

Activity 4.12   Linking to your experience

Take three to five pages of your notes. Jot down for each topic an example from your experience of the point being made: e.g. in chemistry, where have you met that chemical in use?; in geography, where have you seen that land-form?; in English Literature, when have you known a person act like a particular character in a novel?

Activity 4.13   Linking to your past knowledge

Choose a topic which you have recently studied or are about to study. Jot down everything that you already know which you think might link to that topic: e.g. in maths, if you are studying calculus, note down what you know about equations and graphs; in learning a new tense of a foreign language verb, jot down the tenses you already know.

Activity 4.14   Explaining to someone else _____

Take a topic which does not require any very precise prior knowledge. Jot down how you would explain it to someone else. Make a
special note of:

- what you would tell them at the start about what they will learn;
- what order you would present material in;
- what visual aids you would use;
- how you would check that they have understood the topic.

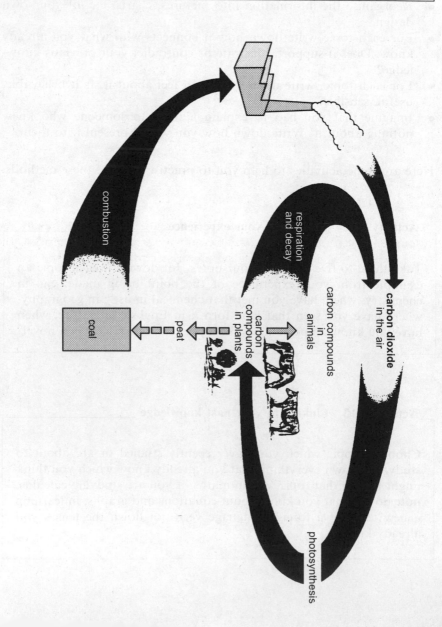

Figure 4.3   The carbon cycle

5 | Memory

5.1 What can you remember?

'I can never remember . . .' We can all complete that sentence with something. For some of us it is names, for others, faces, and for others, numbers. Analysing what you remember easily – and what not – can help you design methods to improve your memory.

Activity 5.1   What you remember

List five types of things that you remember easily and five types which you do not. Choose as wide a range of topics as you can, not restricting yourself to study topics.

To analyse your responses, you are going to score each of your ten topics on two scales. The first scale counts how many characteristics the topic has of things which are generally easier to remember; the second scale counts how many characteristics the topic has of things which are generally harder to remember.

Easier to remember

	Topic (tick)				
Characteristics	1	2	3	4	5
Group A Important to me/need it Like it Use it a lot					
Group B Relaxed when I learn it Learn by doing/using					

77

Group C
Understand it
Material is meaningful
Material is distinctive
Connects with what I know

Total scores

Harder to remember

Characteristics	Topic (tick)				
	1	2	3	4	5
Group A					
Unimportant to me/do not need it					
Dislike topic					
Rarely use it					
Group B					
Tense when I learn it					
Only learn as theory					
Group C					
Can't understand it					
Material not meaningful					
Material not distinctive					
No connection with what I know					
Total scores					

(The two scales are simply the opposite of each other so strictly speaking only one scale is needed. I have put both in to emphasise what the opposite learning conditions are.)

You should find that topics that you find easier to remember produce high scores (6 to 9) on the 'easy-to-remember' scale and low scores (0 to 3) on the 'hard-to-remember scale'. Topics which you find hard to remember will be the reverse of this.

I have divided the scales into three sections which group related factors:

- The **A** group contains motivational factors. If you need or like something, you are well motivated towards it. Motivation helps learning.
- The **B** group deals with the circumstances under which you learn. Learning by doing is always more effective than learning in the abstract. Equally important is being relaxed. Tension interferes with our short-term memory which is why we forget the names of people to whom we are introduced.
- The **C** group covers characteristics of what we are learning. You will already appreciate why meaningful material is easier to learn.

This activity would be of little value if there were no way of moving topics which you find harder to learn into the easier-to-learn category. Fortunately there is a way – or rather a variety of ways – as an examination of the scales in the activity will show you.

To make a topic which you find hard to remember into something which you find easier to remember, you have to look for ways of:

- making it more important to you (e.g. if you are learning a foreign language, go on holiday to the country concerned);
- liking it more;
- using it more;
- being more relaxed whilst learning it;
- learning it in a practical way;
- understanding it better;
- making it more meaningful;
- making the material more distinctive;
- connecting it with what you know.

Much of this is similar to what you have come across already in connection with learning – that should not be surprising since memory and learning are very closely connected.

Activity 5.2 Making things easier to remember

In this activity you are going to work on some examples of things that you find hard to remember but wish that you could remember more easily. You could reuse the 'hard to remember' list from Activity 5.1 or choose some new ones. Select five items. For each one, try to think of what you could do to:

- make the item more important to you;
- learn it in a more practical way;
- make sure that you really understand it.

Topic	Ideas to		
	Increase importance	Make practical	Ensure understanding
1			
2			
3			

5.2   That's odd

Activity 5.3   A memory test

At the end of this book (Appendix A), there is a list of twenty words. Look at the list for exactly one minute, memorising it as best you can. Then close this book and write down as much of the list as you can remember. Take as long as you like to write your list down. When you can recall no more, check how many items you correctly recalled and how many you missed. Keep your list for later on in this chapter.

My guess is that you probably recalled 'encyclopaedia'. Why? The word encyclopaedia stands out in the list in two ways. First, it is the only word with complicated spelling – I had to check it in the dictionary to make sure. Second, it is much longer than any of the other words.

ANYTHING THAT (**STANDS OUT**) IS EASY
TO REMEMBER

Whenever you have to learn a large amount of material that is all very similar, you will find the learning hard. Our brains have evolved over millions of years to be good at 'spot the difference'. It is worth recalling that, genetically speaking, man is a hunter. Hunters need to spot and respond quickly to changes in the environment – the pouncing leopard, the fleeing deer. When nothing changes, the hunter moves to find another spot.

If our brains are no good at learning masses of similar material, we must turn what has to be learnt into distinctive and dissimilar material. We have to increase the discrimination between the items to be learnt. For example, I found it impossible to remember the difference between the French words *dessus* (on top of) and *dessous* (underneath) because they are so similar. I needed some other way to distinguish them. This I found in the fact that *dessous* (underneath) is the longer (bigger) word and larger objects naturally go underneath smaller ones. So I just think of:

dessus

---

dessous

and I can immediately identify the difference.

Activity 5.4   Creating differences

Think of three pairs of things which you find you often confuse with each other. Work out how you can increase the difference between the items and so make them easier to remember.

5.3   That's important

Go back to the list that you wrote in Activity 5.3. Did your list include 'sex'? I expect so. Almost certainly if your name is 'Peter' or 'Alice' – or someone very special to you has one of those names – then your list included them as well.

What this demonstrates is that things which are important to us or are emotive are easily remembered. You could say that we always remember what we really want to remember. What we forget is not important to us.

This may sound odd. After all, passing an exam may be important so why don't we easily remember all the course work for the exam? The answer lies in the fact that what is important to us is the possession of the exam pass, not the course material itself.

Somehow we have to find ways of making the material more important to ourselves. Once you have found a way of becoming interested in the topics themselves – and not just in the exam pass – remembering the material will become much easier. There are many ways to achieve this:

- Applying the learning to a practical problem.
- Helping others to learn it – explaining something difficult to someone else is a very powerful way of promoting your own understanding.
- Agreeing in advance to make a presentation on a topic to friends or colleagues – you will work with much more enthusiasm.
- Discussing the topic with a colleague – the act of discussion creates enthusiasm.

Activity 5.5   Making material important

Either

Look through your study programme for the next few weeks. Decide what you will do to study the material in a way which will increase its importance to you.

Or

Look back over what you have studied in the past two weeks and identify what you could have done – or could still do – to increase the importance of the material to you.

5.4   Beginnings and ends

Once more, look back at the list that you wrote down in Activity 5.3. There is a very good chance that your list includes 'table' and 'spoon'. This is because we tend to remember beginnings and ends. (We can often recall the first and last lines of poems, but nothing else.)

We more easily remember beginnings and ends because of the state of our minds at that those points. At the start of the list, our minds are clear. No other learning is being attempted. As a result, our full attention is on the first item on the list – there is nothing to interfere with our committing it to memory. Similarly, when we come to the last item on the list, because it is the last, nothing follows it to interfere with its being remembered.

What this tells us is that it is important to split up what is to be learnt into small chunks so that we create lots of beginnings and ends.

Activity 5.6 Learning a list again

Appendix B (don't look yet) contains another twenty words but this time laid out as four lists of five words each. You again have exactly one minute to attempt to memorise the twenty words. This time, treat the words as four lists, trying to learn each one by itself. After the one minute, close this book and write down as many words as you can remember.

With luck you will have remembered more because there are more beginnings and ends – eight instead of two.

What you have just demonstrated has to be interpreted with care. After all, you do not spend much time learning lists. Most of what you learn is more complex and involves more application. But still the general principle applies: learn in small chunks.

Here are some examples of how you might split up what you have to learn.

Chapter of a book
Divide the chapter into sections, each with one main new idea. Work on each section as if it were all that you had to learn. For example, you might apply SQ3R (see Chapter 4) to one section at a time. Do not leave the section until you have mastered it. Ideally have a break between sections.

Concentrated topics
E.g. formulae, scientific laws, foreign-language verb tenses or grammatical rules, complex processes and procedures. Treat the one item as all that is to be learnt – put everything else to one side. Examine your topic. How can it be subdivided into distinct parts on which you can concentrate individually (these become like beginnings and ends)? For example, for a formula, you might separate it into: the assumptions

behind the formula, what the variables mean, when to use the formula, when not to use it, how to rearrange it, related formulae and so on. For a verb tense, you might divide its study into: the English equivalent, when to use it in the foreign language, when not to use it, how the endings work, tenses with which it might be confused, endings of other tenses that might be confused with it.

There is no right way, but the better you are at splitting material up so as to concentrate on each aspect, the better your recall will be.

Stop interfering

A lot of what I have said in the last few pages has been based on lists. Fortunately, most learning has little to do with lists. You have seen that where material has associations with what you already know and is meaningful to you, learning is enhanced. There is one final aspect of list-learning to consider and to explore how far it applies to other forms of learning. That is interference.

If (it is too late now) I had asked you learn the list in Appendix B straight after that in Appendix A, you would have found that your recall of the A list would have affected the recall of the B list. You would have confused the two lists.

Does this mean that every study period risks interfering with the previous one? The answer is 'No', but 'No' with some conditions.

If you attempt to learn material by rote – that is, if you treat your course like a long list to be remembered – then each new study-period will tend to interfere with its predecessor. Just when you thought you had remembered something, the next learning-point weakens your recall of the previous one.

But, surprisingly, exactly the reverse happens if you really try to understand what you are learning. If you learn topic A and then move on to topic B, you can use topic B to help to reinforce your recall and understanding of A. All you have to do is to look for links (or contrasts) between topic B and what you learnt in A. This active recall and link building reinforces your learning of both topics.

Activity 5.7   Linking topics

Look through what you have been working on over the last few weeks, noting up to five topics that you have studied. Make sure you keep them in the order in which you previously studied them. For each topic after the first, jot down some ideas on what links you could have made between it and the previous topic.

5.5   Multiple connections

No simple model adequately describes human memory. It has characteristics of many models and each can help us to understand more about how we learn. One valuable model is that of associations. Once again, lists are a good starting-point. Appendix A started:

> table
> car
> music

The normal way to learn the list in order is by rote. Having succeeded, each word becomes linked to its predecessor:

> table → car → music

The word 'car' is associated with 'table' so that recalling 'table' helps us to recall 'car'. But what happens if we cannot recall 'table'? Usually it means that we cannot recall 'car' either. The one word triggers the other. This demonstrates why it is so hard to learn lists. Whenever what we try to remember is associated with only one other item in our minds, the risk of forgetting is greatly increased. Robust memory depends on multiple associations.

Consider something that we might remember really well – say a favourite television programme. Its title may well be linked to dozens of other ideas as illustrated in Figure 5.1.

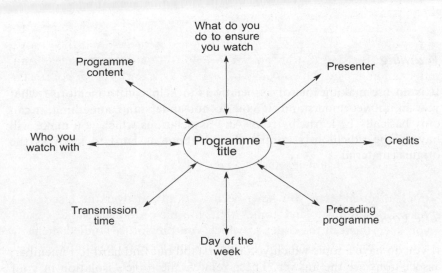

Figure 5.1   Possible associations for a TV programme title

Any one of the associated ideas might trigger recall of the programme title. More importantly, should you forget one of the associated ideas, you still have plenty of others to help you to recall the title.

Activity 5.8   Single association items

Make a list of five items which you currently find very hard to remember, e.g. a car registration number. For each, try to think of three items with which you could associate what you wish to remember.

Activity 5.9   Noting associations

Associations are even more powerful aids to memory if they are specially noted. (The act of recall and noting presumably strengthens the link.) Try to identify some existing associations which you have made in your learning. Take five very different items (e.g. where you live, a favourite piece of music) and try to identify three other things that you associate with each.

Warning

It is no use making lots of associations to help you to memorise what you do not yet understand. If you do not understand something, it can only basically be learnt by rote. Any associations which you make will have to be ridiculously contrived and about as hard to learn as the original material.

The good news

If you do have a topic which you understand but find hard to remember, associations are the answer. These remove the topic's isolation in your brain.

Summary on links and associations

Basically there are three approaches to remembering. These are summarised in Figures 5.2, 5.3 and 5.4.

In Figure 5.2, the single link per item shows how easy it is to forget an item acquired by rote learning:

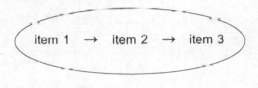

Figure 5.2   Rote learning

Figure 5.3 shows a better approach where for each topic the learner builds multiple links. However there are still no links between topics so recall here will be good but not as good as it could be.

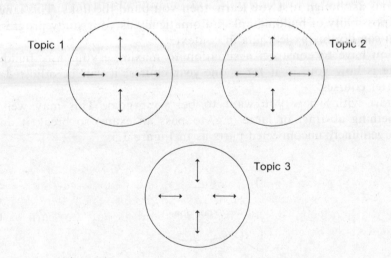

Figure 5.3   Associations built within topics

For maximum possible recall, the associations need to be built within and between topics. This is demonstrated in Figure 5.4.

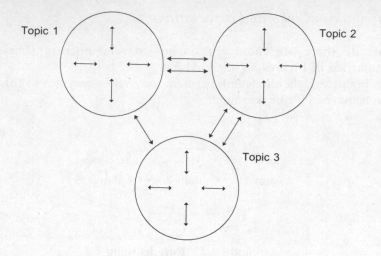

Figure 5.4   Associations within and between topics

5.6   Context is all

What I have said so far about making links is slightly artificial. It all sounds as though first you learn, then you build the links. This ignores the possibility of building links automatically as your study progresses. You can do this by learning in context.

You have to construct a situation to maximise your link building. Here is how you do it for a one-year course; it can be adjusted for shorter courses.

Start with where you want to be: your goal. This may well be something abstract or large (e.g. to pass an exam) so break it down into genuinely unconnected parts as in Figure 5.5.

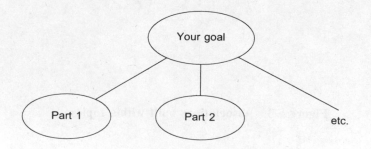

Figure 5.5   Your goal in parts

Now think of what you wish to be able to do within each part. Avoid saying 'To know . . .' or 'To understand . . .'. Instead describe something more active such as 'To solve . . .' or 'To design . . .'. So you now have Figure 5.6.

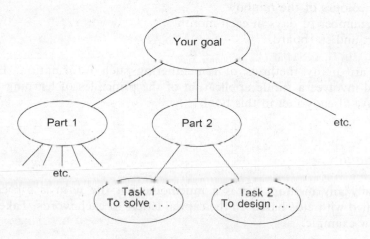

Figure 5.6   Subgoals identified

What you now have is a series of tasks which represent the purpose of your learning – not what you intend to learn but what you intend to do with the learning. Your tasks will draw on a much wider range of ideas and knowledge than the strict content of your course. By working towards these tasks, you will build a very wide range of links.

Activity 5.10   Identifying a context

Take a part of your study programme. Try to put it into context by describing some tasks that you hope to achieve.

5.7   Rote learning – when you cannot avoid it

You have already attempted the learning of two arbitrary lists of words. This should have been a painful or boring reminder of how difficult rote learning is. Throughout this book I have stressed the value of not learning by rote. I have stressed that the key to successful learning lies in the context, in making material meaningful and in using it actively. Despite all this, we are sometimes left with a rump of material which does not fit any of these learning methods. Such material has to be learnt by rote.

The essential characteristic of what has to be learnt by rote is its arbitrariness – it has no meaning or pattern. Examples are:

● the colours of the rainbow
● the number of days in each month
● port and starboard.

There are many methods of remembering such information. Each method involves a subtle application of the principles of learning that you have already met in this book.

Mnemonics

Generally any memory aid is a mnemonic but the term is especially associated with aids based on the capital letters of each words. Take the rainbow example:

Red	
Orange	Arbitrary
Yellow	information
Green	– difficult to
Blue	remember
Indigo	
Violet	
ROYGBIV	Extract its initial letters
Richard Of York Gave	Associate the initial letters
Battle In Vain	with an easy to remember phrase

This method uses the power of association and of a meaningful phrase to help to remember what was initially a meaningless list. Its power is totally dependent on the phrase that you choose being both meaningful and striking to you. So the best mnemonics are often the ones which you make up for yourself.

Verbal associations

Here the items to be remembered are associated with something which is already well-known. For example, many of us have difficulty in remembering which is left and right of port and starboard, and which of them is the red and the green. Assuming that you know that port wine is red and traditionally drunk after a meal, then the phrase:

port is red and left to after dinner

will instantly remind you that port is the left-hand side and has a red light; starboard must therefore be the right-hand side and green in colour.

The method works through the power of associating something new and strange with something that is very well-embedded in your mind. As with mnemonics it is best to choose associations that are vivid and meaningful to you. If you cannot recall that port is drunk after dinner, the foregoing association is useless to you.

6 Written work

6.1 Keep it in style

If you got up one morning to find a letter on your doormat from a close friend, you would not have to open it to guess at its style. You would know in advance that it would not read like a letter from a lawyer, the *Sun* front page or a dictionary of philosophy. Each type of document has its own writing style, chosen most deliberately by its authors.

In study, choosing the right style is just as important. You will need a style for rough notes, one for complete notes, one for short-answer questions, one for essays and so on. Being able to switch styles is an important part of the writing side of study. The more easily you can do it, the more comfortable you will be with the study process.

Activity 6.1   Your current styles

Look back over your last four weeks' work and identify the various styles of written work that you have had to do. For each, list the essential features of that style when you have used it.

Why should you bother with style? There are three good reasons:

- the right style makes the content clearer;
- the right style is easier to use than the wrong one;
- your readers expect you to use the right style.

I shall look at each of these in turn.

- When the style matches the content, the content becomes clearer to the reader. For example, when material is in note form, that form emphasises key points and relationships – just what you want notes to do. When something is in essay form, the sequence and coherence of the sustained argument is highlighted – that is the purpose of an essay. But when style fails to match content, the reader is aware that 'something is wrong' and your message or purpose suffers as a result.
- Style, too, can ease the writing burden. With a well-chosen style, the content and the form support each other so that deciding what you

92

want to say effectively decides how you are going to say it. Imagine how difficult it would be if you were asked to write notes in essay form.

- Finally, it always helps to remember what your audience will expect. Tutors and examiners expect essays to be in a certain form. To submit an essay in any other form than that expected would only lead to its rejection.

Activity 6.2 Analysing your current styles

In this chapter I am going to discuss a number of writing styles, emphasising how they differ from each other. Before doing so, you might find it useful to review your own writing styles in order to explore how consistent and distinct each is. For this activity, you need to consider your writing in the categories below. For each category, try to identify how you use the style. Which features does your essay writing include and which does it exclude?

Style	Includes	Excludes
Short answer		
Without words (i.e. diagrams, etc.)		
Reports		
Presenting a case		
Essays		
Projects		

The point of this activity is to assist you in analysing how distinctly and consistently you use each style. Do you mix styles within one piece of work? Do you maintain a distinct difference between a report and an essay? Where you are unsure of what the differences ought to be, or feel that you cannot maintain distinct styles, the rest of this chapter will help you.

You will be able to use what follows in two ways:

- to keep to a prescribed style;
- to choose an appropriate style.

Both situations arise in study. Sometimes a prescribed task – especially when it is an assessment or exam – is very precise about the required answer format. This chapter will help you to keep to that. At other times, you have a task to do – perhaps self-prescribed. Choosing for yourself an appropriate style always makes the task easier. This chapter will help you with that too.

6.2   Short answers

Students are often asked to answer questions in a short-answer format. There is no one way of showing that this might be the required format, but it will be indicated somewhere within the question or in the way that the question is given to you. Ways of indicating that this is the desired format include:

- Describe in up to 200 words . . .
- List the five main reasons why . . .
- What are the essential features of . . .?
- Or, you may be given an answer sheet which only has enough space for a short answer.

There will always be a good reason for the choice of this format by the tutor or examiner. If you look carefully, you should be able to identify the reason which will then help you to answer in the most efficient and effective way.

Effective and efficient

Whether it is short answer or any of the other forms which I shall be discussing, you need to be effective and efficient. What do I mean by this? Being effective means that you meet the purpose behind the question. You give the right information, make the appropriate points, etc. Everything which you put down is relevant and necessary. Nothing is missing. Being efficient means that you do this with the least possible effort. Your answer will be the shortest which does the job well and avoids any unnecessary material.

So, a short-answer question requires an efficient and effective answer. This requires you to spot just what the answer needs to contain – no more, no less – and to present that succinctly. To decide how to answer such a question, ask:

- What points must the answer contain?
- How can those points be presented concisely?

Activity 6.3 Short-answer formats

Here are a variety of short-answer question wordings. For each, identify what the answer will need to contain and in what format the answer will need to be.

Question wording	Points to include	Form of answer
1. List three examples of . . .		
2. Describe . . .		
3. Give five main reasons why . . .		
4. Explain		
5. Describe the steps you would take to . . .		
6. Give an account of how you would . . .		

A precise answer will naturally depend on the exact wording of the question, but as a rough guide, here are my responses:

Question	Points to include	Form of answer
1.	The three examples	As a list 1, 2, 3
2.	The facts	As a paragraph
3.	The five reasons	As a list 1, 2, 3, 4, 5
4.	The reasons which make up the explanation	List or paragraph
5.	The steps, in order with a little detail on each	List or paragraph
6.	A set of points, in order	List or paragraph

In three cases I have said 'list or paragraph'. Judging which is best is partly a matter of judging the preference of your tutor, assessor, etc. I am very keen on lists because of their clarity, but not all tutors take the same view.

Short-answer summary

To continue with my preference, I will summarise this section as a list. Short answers should:

- contain exactly the points needed;
- be organised to use the minimum time to make your points clear;
- follow any format requirements of the question (e.g. 'list . . .', 'give three reasons . . .').

Short answers may be:

- lists;
- use phrases rather than full sentences;
- require whole paragraphs.

6.3   Without words

Well, almost no words, since this section is about the use of diagrams, charts, etc. in answers. 'A picture is worth a thousand words' is a popular cliché and, in general, a picture or a diagram is better than words when you want to show how something is. Our brains can absorb more information more quickly in visual format, especially when the picture has been designed to promote learning.

An examination of some of the things which pictures are particularly good at immediately suggests when and when not to use them. Pictures and diagrams can:

- show colour;
- show shape and size;
- show how something should be constructed;
- show physical relationships (e.g. a map);
- show movement (through a series of pictures) (e.g. how a car engine works);
- show the order in which something occurs or should be done;
- show how to do something practical;
- show cause and effect.

Most of these are near to impossible to do with words. Of the above items, only 'show order' could be done with words by using a list.

Equally we need to be clear about what diagrams and pictures are not good at. They cannot:

- present an argument;
- make a case;
- evaluate;
- reach conclusions;
- deal with abstract concepts (e.g. goodness, freedom);
- deal with sound.

Making effective use of pictures and diagrams is just as important in your general study as in your assessment activities. Indeed unless you have developed lots of ideas on how to use diagrams, they will not come to you easily when you want them later on. So the next activity gets you to take a look at how well you use diagrams at present.

___ **Activity 6.4   Your use of diagrams** _____

Look through your notes or other personal work of the last few weeks. Try to find at least one example of each of the following content types. Did you make the best possible use of diagrams? If not, set out your ideas on how you could have been more effective in your use of diagrams.

Content type	*How a diagram would help*
Show colour	
Show shape and size	
Show method of construction	
Show physical relationships	
Show movement	
Show order of tasks	
Show how to do something	
Show cause and effect	

6.4   Reports

As I have emphasised, form and content go together. You have only to consider the purpose of a particular format to gain a fairly clear idea of how it should be presented.

Reports have two main functions:

- to establish the facts
- to enable a decision to be made.

Activity 6.5 The contents of reports

Consider the following examples of reports. Identify in each case the sort of facts that would be included and the decision that would be made as a result of the report.

Report	Facts	Decision(s)
Ship sinking with loss of life		
Prisoner applying for parole		
Surveyor's report on a house		
Doctor's report on a patient		

Here are my ideas on this activity.

Report	Facts	Decision(s)
Ship sinking with loss of life	Events leading up to sinking Who did what, when Who knew what	Whether to prosecute Insurance pay-out Whether to amend legislation
Prisoner applying for parole	Past behaviour Support available outside Statistics of similar offenders in the past	Whether to grant parole How to monitor the parole
Surveyor's report on a house	Repairs needed Likely future faults Value	Whether to purchase What price to pay
Doctor's report on a patient	History of illness Past treatment Progress of other similar patients in past	Options for treatment Prognosis to give patient

The key point that all this illustrates is that the contents of a report are determined solely by the proposed use of the report. If I want to decide whether to buy a house, a surveyor's report should cover only those facts that are relevant to my decision.

This simple rule – purpose determines content – does not make report-writing trivially simple. For a start, it can be difficult to decide in advance which facts will prove relevant to the decision. The more standard a report (like the surveyor's house report), the easier it is to predict the contents needed. But suppose that you were asked to prepare a report on the likely costs and benefits of building a new road. Do you consider the local environmental effects, contribution to the greenhouse effect, voters' views, etc.?

Structure of a report

Writing a report is straightforward but requires strong discipline – it is as much about leaving out material as putting it in. A well-structured report will be something like:

- *The remit* – who asked you to prepare the report; what the brief was and what the purpose was.
- *Summary* – not all your readers will have time to read the full report, so provide a clear summary which concentrates on the conclusions and recommendations.
- *Your approach* – what information you decided to collect, how you collected it, from whom, etc.
- *The facts* – what you found out. This needs careful structuring into sections which cover individual topics. Clear numbering and generous headings help.
- *Conclusions* – an assessment of what the report found out. Here you might draw attention to facts that could not be established or where you found conflicting evidence.
- *Recommendations* – remind your readers of the purpose of the report and set out what decisions you think should be made given the evidence that you found.

6.5 Making a case

This category of writing lies somewhere between report-writing and essay-writing. Here you are putting forward a point of view in a more committed way than in a report. It is a more personal document. You may also put forward a point of view in an essay but an essay tends to be more formal and discursive. As an example, you might be writing about word processors in offices. As a report, an argued case or an essay, this might successively appear as:

Report	An investigation of the value of word processors in offices.
Case	The case for our office to buy word processors.
Essay	Word processors are essential in today's offices. Discuss.

From here on, this section will only discuss 'making a case'.

People commonly make the mistake of attempting to make a case by putting forward all possible arguments in its favour. This sometimes works, but it always runs the risk of not sounding credible. Almost always the reader will be aware of some arguments against the case. If these have been ignored, the case will seem flawed. There must be a better way.

You can find the better way by thinking what a case needs to do if it is to be unassailable. Basically a case is convincing only when all the evidence against it has been shown to be outweighed by the evidence in favour of the case. This sets the agenda for making a case.

Assumptions

The evidence, however, is not the starting point. That is your assumptions. No case can be made in a void. Every case is made against a background of values and assumptions that, in effect, determine which evidence will be considered valuable or relevant.

Activity 6.6   Assumptions behind a case

Imagine that you have been asked to make the cases below. What assumptions would you have to make before starting on each one?

Case	Assumptions
Putting fluoride in public water supplies	
Building a road which is bound to involve demolishing some houses	
Moving a factory from London to Birmingham	

Here are the assumptions that I thought would have to be made.

Case	Assumptions
Putting fluoride in public water supplies	That, in principle, governments have the right to add chemicals to the public water supply
Building a road which is bound to involve demolishing some houses	That, in principle, public authorities may compulsorily purchase private property
Moving a factory from London to Birmingham	That the factory should not be closed or split up

This last example illustrates how important it is to state your assumptions clearly since, in effect, they restrict the case or cases that you will consider.

Criteria

Having set down your assumptions, you next need to set down your criteria for assessing the evidence. How will you decide the balance of the arguments for and against? Examples of criteria that you might set are:

- If at least 100 people benefit for each person who suffers, I will accept the case.
- If the benefits are worth at least 10 per cent of one year's profits, I will consider the case proved.

Activity 6.7   Criteria

Write down some criteria for the cases you considered in Activity 6.6.

Case	Criteria
Fluoride	
Road building	
Factory move	

The arguments

You now have your assumptions and your criteria. Next you must set out the evidence for and against the case.

Evaluation

Having set out the evidence, you must evaluate it – that is, weigh the points in favour against those against. It is important to do this using only the criteria that you set out at the beginning of your report. If you change your criteria or add to them at this stage, it will look as if you are fixing the argument rather than letting the facts speak for themselves.

Conclusions

Finally, you reach your conclusions which will:

- restate the case you set out to establish;
- remind the reader of your assumptions;
- remind the reader of your criteria;
- summarise how the evidence, on balance, supports your case.

Putting a case – summary
   To recap, the steps in making a case are:

- state your assumptions;
- state your criteria;
- set out the evidence;
- evaluate the evidence;
- set out your conclusions.

6.6   Writing essays

Essays are perhaps the most feared part of study. Many people find that they are unable to start essays. Others make a start but find themselves unable to finish. Yet, when you look closely at what an essay involves, there is no special skill which you would not practise elsewhere in your study. This leads me to suppose that there are two reasons why students consider essays to be difficult. First, the very word 'essay' has a mystique about it. Second, essays are comparatively lengthy and so it is the scale of the task that deters. The first problem is easily put into perspective by remembering that the word 'essay' comes from the French verb *essayer* (to try) so an essay is literally 'an attempt'. Who could think of 'an attempt' as having any mystique? The second problem – length – is easily dealt with by the usual method for approaching any big task, that is, to break it down into small tasks. This section will look at that process in more detail.

Activity 6.8   How do you write essays?

Think about an essay which you have recently written. Write down the process which you went through from first looking at the title to finishing the task. Consider whether your process for this essay is typical of that for the other essays which you have written.

Your process

How typical for you?

Perhaps now that you have reflected on your own essay-writing process, you have found that you are quite systematic. In case you are not, I shall now look at what makes an essay and how you can approach its writing in a systematic manner.

The essay

An essay is usually a discussion of a statement or proposition. It requires you to take a viewpoint and to argue that viewpoint in essay format. Traditionally essays are expected to come in three parts but I shall list four:

- title;
- introduction;
- main argument;
- conclusions.

(My fourth part is the title. Given its importance in determining how you write the essay, I feel that it must be listed alongside the other three parts. See Figure 6.1.)

The title

Essay titles are always carefully chosen. Usually the basic topic is broad, but one or two key words in the title narrow the essay's scope. Consider these titles as examples:

- The threat to the environment can only be reduced by economic growth. Discuss.
- Are wage increases the main cause of inflation?

Students often read titles such as these and conclude that they are being asked to write as much as they know on 'the environment', 'economic growth', 'wage increases' or 'inflation'. In fact, you do not need to write much about any of these topics. What the first title asks you to do is to identify the most probable ways of reducing the threat to the environment and then to assess whether economic growth is more effective than any of the other options.

The title determines what is going to be relevant to the essay and what is not.

The introduction

In your introduction you essentially set how you are going to tackle the essay. (There is, after all, no one correct way.) You may have to write about:

- how you interpret the terms in the title (e.g. what you understand by 'the threat to the environment');
- any assumptions that you are going to make rather than argue in detail;
- what criteria you are going to use to reach your conclusions. (e.g. you might say 'the environment is so important that I shall assume that anything which has an unknown effect must be assumed to have a bad effect');
- how you are going to structure your essay.

In writing your introduction it is important to remember that almost any approach can gain high marks provided that:

- the approach is consistent with the title;
- you justify that approach in your introduction.

The main argument

This is the largest part of the essay and the part where it is easiest to get carried away. Many students simply write down all they know on what they take to be the topic. In practice, very little knowledge may be needed.

Essentially, in the main argument, you are making one or more propositions. You have to justify these by relevant examples and you have to show that you have taken account of any apparently conflicting evidence. The process is very similar to 'making a case' discussed in 6.5. Your work will be judged on the aptness of your examples and how thoroughly you have dealt with any evidence against your case.

The conclusions

Essays do not have summaries but conclusions. 'Conclusions' and 'summary' are not the same thing. What your conclusion should do is to bring your whole argument (including the introduction) together into a set of points that you want your reader to retain. You can think of it as the output of the essay process.

The title	=	Your starting orders
Introduction	=	Setting the scene
		Establishing your approach
Main argument	=	Your propositions
		and evidence
Conclusions	=	What you want the reader
		to take away

Figure 6.1   The parts of an essay

Writing the essay

I said earlier that it is the scale of an essay which seems to daunt students. That is a natural reaction to any big task. Fortunately there is a very well-proven method of tackling large projects which makes them lose their largeness: break them down into a series of small tasks. Here is one method of breaking an essay down.

Step 1   Analyse the title

- Ask yourself: what does each word mean? What is the link between the words?
- Make a list of what has to be covered to fit the title.
- Make a list of points that the title allows you to leave out.

Step 2   Consider possible approaches

- Jot down as many approaches to the essay as you can think of.
- Decide which approach seems best for you.

Step 3   Collect ideas

- Make a list of all the points that you might make.

Step 4   Decide on a structure

- The best way to do this is to use the nuclear notes format discussed in Chapter 4 (4.4). Put the title at the centre; then use one main branch for each main point that you wish to make (Figure 6.2).

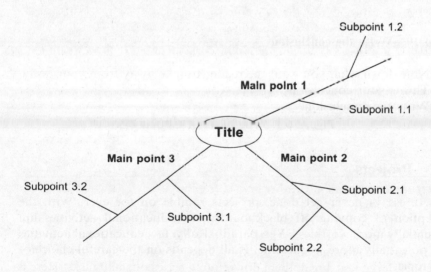

Figure 6.2   Nuclear notes for an essay

Step 5   Decide on an order

- Review your nuclear notes and decide on the order in which you will discuss the points.

Step 6   Collect the evidence

● List your main points from Step 5. Then against each point, jot down the evidence that you will use in support of it and any evidence against which you will need to discuss.

Step 7   Outline the introduction

● Now that you have decided your argument, note down what your reader will need to know before reading the main part of your essay. This is your introduction.

Step 8   Write the introduction

Step 9   Write the main argument

● Work through the contents of the table in Step 6, point by point.

Step 10   Write the conclusion

● Note down what you want the reader to take away from your essay. This is your conclusion.
● Write the conclusion.

6.7   Projects

Where essays never get done, projects ramble on for ever. With the exception of copying off blackboards, few educational activities are potentially more worthless. Yet, paradoxically, few educational activities are potentially more worthwhile. It all depends on the careful choice of the topic.

Projects such as 'India' or 'Fishing' seem to me to be impossible to do well, or to finish. They are so vast as to have no bounds and no aims. Other projects such as 'To devise ways of reducing food waste in our canteen by 10 per cent' or 'An investigation of factors which affect the efficiency of garden compost bins' are much better bounded and have a more obvious end-point. You know when you have written enough: when you have dealt with the problem in the title.

My point in these introductory remarks is to warn you that this section will be of only limited help in completing projects with daft titles.

A successful project requires a sensible title, and what that is I shall discuss shortly.

Stage 1 Choosing a title

Activity 6.9 Examining your project titles

Find some projects that you have done in the past – or ones that you might have to do in the future. Examine the titles carefully to identify in what way the content was/is limited by the title and in what way the aim of the project was/is specified.

If you reached the conclusion that some of these projects were badly defined, try rewriting their specifications more tightly. Use the following as a format to help your thinking:

- Topic: what is the broad topic to be?
- Limits: in what ways will you limit the content?
- Aims: what precise outcomes would you expect of a successful project on this topic and with these limits?

Activity 6.10 Choosing a topic

This activity should help you to appreciate that choosing the right title is a key part in writing a successful project. The rest of this section will involve activities built around a topic of your choosing. Select a topic now which you can use for this.

Stage 2 Research – collecting ideas

Before you can go off and research your project, you have to have a fairly good idea of what information you want. Often, the sources that you will consult (e.g. encyclopaedias and reference books) will be full of material that is irrelevant to your topic. So you will have to scan (see Chapter 4) to locate what is relevant to you. Scanning is much more effective if you have specific questions to which you are seeking answers.

For this reason, a good way to plan your research is to write down a whole series of questions to which you want answers. To generate the questions, try this two stage approach:

- Think hard for 30 minutes to 1 hour to collect as many questions as possible, i.e. take a blank sheet of paper and write down any question that comes into your head without stopping to evaluate it. Just trap as many ideas as possible.
- ˙ Organise the questions into some sensible order, e.g. by subtopic or by date, or whatever makes sense to you.
- Evaluate the questions, removing duplicates and ones which don't really seem essential to the project.

Activity 6.11   Brainstorming

For your topic, write down as many ideas as possible in five to ten minutes to generate possible questions. Organise your questions in the format below.

Topic:

Sub-topic	Questions to research

Stage 3   Research – sources
Now that you have the questions your next need is to find out where the answers might come from. There are three major types of source:

- published material (books, videos, newspapers, electronic databases etc.);
- people;
- your own observations, (measurements, experiments, etc.).

At this stage in a project, you are faced with the task of deciding which sources will help with which questions. Unless you know some remarkably helpful people, or have endless time for observation, it is probably best to check the published material first.

Except for very specialised research or something too topical to be in books, the following method should give you the sources which you need:

- Check through two good general books on your subject, making sure that you choose books with good bibliographies.
- Take a piece of card headed 'general issues' and note down which of your questions can be covered from these general works.
- For each question which cannot be answered by the general works, take one piece of card and write the question at the top. Then using the bibliograpies from your two books, note on each card the details of those more specialised books that look as if they will deal with your questions

For very topical material you will need to use a good newspaper index or an on-line database which allows you to search newspapers and journals. For very specialised material, you will need to consult professional journals.

You now have sources against each question. (If you have the odd blank, don't worry, your other research will soon turn up a source for this.)

Activity 6.12   Finding sources

For your topic, find one or two general books and start building a list of sources.

Now list more specialised sources for your questions:

Question number	Source(s)
1.	
2.	
3.	

Stage 4   Research – extracting information

You have now found sources for all (or almost all) of your questions and are ready to extract the information that you need. Here is what to do:

- For each question, take a large file-card or sheet of paper.
- Write the question at the top of the card.

- Scan the sources for relevant material.
- When you find relevant material, write down notes about it on the card. Remember to note down the source and the page number.
- You should avoid copying out detailed material. Try to confine your copying to:
  (i)   key quotations;
  (ii) diagrams, tables, etc., where a summary does not make sense.

Stage 5   Planning the writing
By this time you will have a very good understanding of the topic. This will help in planning a structure for your topic. You can use nuclear notes to plan your project – just as in the previous section on essay planning – or you can use the approach that I described in the section on objective setting in Chapter 1. This time I will use the method from Chapter 1. The idea is to plan in successive stages of detail:

- Write down the title of each section or chapter.
- For each section, write down the topics that you will cover in the order that you propose.
- For each topic, write down the points that you will include. Each of these points might well correspond to one paragraph when you start the full writing.
- Now the outline is complete.

This planning process is summarised in Figure 6.3.

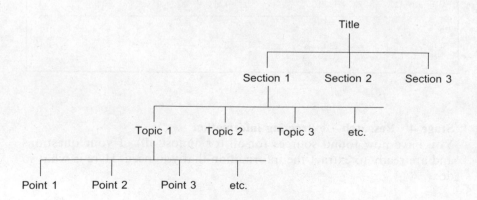

Figure 6.3   Project planning

Activity 6.13   Writing a project outline

For the project which you worked on in Activity 6.12, try the above method to draw up an outline.

Step 6   Writing

Start with point one of topic one and work steadily through your outline. If your cards are well planned, the material that you need at each point will be on one card. Look at the information on the card, and write in your own words what you wish to say. Ask whether what you have written is:

- strictly relevant to your project title?
- in your own words? (Except for necessary quotations.)
- well-placed in the overall order of the project?
- well-linked to the previous section?
- at the right level of detail?

Stage 7   Review and edit

No one can write a finished effort at the first draft. Once you have written your project, read it through to see how it flows. Does it read like a single coherent piece, or does it have gaps and messy joins? Decide where to cut and where to add more material.

Only when all your content is complete should you come back and do a final edit, looking for spelling mistakes, poor sentence structure and so on. This final polish removes all those tiny imperfections which leads even the best-argued piece to give a bad impression.

7 Assessment and exams

7.1 Types of test

There is a popular view that exams and assessments are designed to trick
you into showing how little you know or can do. In fact, even the worst
designed exam is meant to give you a chance to show what you can do.
Very rarely are there any penalties for making mistakes. In this section I
want to look at how you can use assessment in a positive manner – to
get the results which you want.

Activity 7.1   Your experience of assessment

Look back over as many major exams and tests as you can
remember. Include tests such as the driving test and medical
examinations. Work out what you thought the purpose of the test
was (a) from the examiner's point of view and (b) from your point
of view.

You should find from this activity that tests can have many different
purposes.

Mastery tests

These are tests which have to be passed without any mistakes. They are
designed to show that you know or can do something completely. The
driving test is a good example. It is no use having drivers who can do
four out of five things safely when they are highly dangerous performing
the fifth. I would hope – but do not know – that surgeons have to take
mastery tests. Mastery tests are usually the basis of some critical
decision, e.g. is this person safe to drive?

114

Profiles

Profiles simply record what you can do but make no mention of what you are not able to do. Usually with a profile test, you decide when you are ready to demonstrate that you have learnt a new item. Mutliplication tables are often assessed in this way at school. When pupils feel that they have mastered, say, the seven-times table, they present themselves for testing. If they are successful then the seven-times table is ticked off on their profiles.

Formative tests

These are designed to help you learn by giving you comments on what you are and are not able to do. They form your learning. The idea is that you take action on the result of the test. For example, if you test your own vocabulary in a foreign language in order to find out which words you still need to learn, then that is a formative test.

Summative tests

Finally, some tests – called summative tests – summarise what you know or can do at a particular time. Most exams are like this. Their main purpose is to enable future decisions to be made.

It is important to know which type of test you are taking since that affects how you prepare for it. I shall look at preparation shortly.

Test type summary

Test type	Follow-on action
Mastery	Usually you are now permitted to carry out some restricted activity, e.g. driving
Profile	No particular action. You just keep adding to your profile
Formative	Learn the items which you did not know/could not do
Summative	To decide what you will do next, e.g. whether you are eligible for a higher education course

---

Activity 7.2　How you have used tests _____

Review the tests which you listed in Activity 7.1, putting them into the four categories below. Work out what you did with the results of each. Was each well matched for the action or decision which needed to be taken?

Test type	Your tests	Your action
Mastery		
Profile		
Formative		
Summative		

7.2　Preparing for assessment

Activity 7.3　Your past preparation _____

Look back at how you have prepared for tests in the past. List the methods which you used and assess how effective these were for you.

The best method of preparation depends on the content of the test. For the purposes of this section, I am going to look at three broad categories of test: largely knowledge recall; largely applying knowledge (e.g. problem solving or essay writing); and largely practical skills.

Preparing for knowledge-based tests

This type of preparation follows the pursuit of the principles set out in Chapters 3 and 5. Effective recall of knowledge depends on its having been learnt in a meaningful way in the first place.

I shall start with the negative:

Do not sit down and endlessly read through your notes. As you will appreciate by now, that is not an effective learning technique.

Do:

- Make sure that your notes are organised to:
  - (a)   make everything meaningful,
  - (b)   highlight key points;
  - (c)   show structures and relationships;
  - (d)   emphasise differences.

(The techniques for this are all in Chapter 6.)

REMEMBER: MAKE IT MEANINGFUL

- Test yourself (or use a friend) to identify what you know well – put that to one side.
- Take the material that you do not know well and practise using it, e.g. through:
  - (a)   solving problems,
  - (b)   answering past exam questions;
  - (c)   inventing your own questions to answer;
  - (d)   sketching answers to essays;
  - (e)   explaining the item to an imaginary audience.

REMEMBER: MAKE LEARNING ACTIVE

Preparing for application tests

With this type of test there are few, if any, marks for showing that you know the facts. The marks are for showing that you know how to select and use the facts. Clearly you cannot do this unless you know the facts in the first place, so all that I have said in the previous section – and more – applies.

The 'more' is about practising the selection and use of the knowledge. Correct selection is critical in maths and sciences since, if you select the wrong formula or process, your answer will be totally irrelevant and worth few or no marks. Appropriate selection is critical in essay-based subjects since you cannot hope to answer questions in the allocated time unless you are highly selective about the facts that you include.

So practising selection is very important. For problem-solving type of questions, you should:

- Find books with masses of problems (many revision books, especially those published in the USA are ideal for this).
- Without working out detailed solutions, practise looking at questions and jotting down which formulae and processes are needed.
- When it is hard to distinguish whether to use formula A or B, or method A or B, examine the question carefully for what helps you to decide. Make a note of this.
- Finally, practise solving lots of problems.

In essay-type subjects, practising selection involves sketching lots of essay outlines without writing the full essay.

- Find books, past papers, etc., with lots of essay topics – or invent your own.
- For each topic, practise steps 1 to 4 of 'essay writing' from Chapter 6.

Preparing for practical tests

Here I am talking about tests such as art practical exams, typing tests and bricklaying tests. In each case you have to produce something, usually within a given time. As with all other types of test, it is very important to know what form the test will take. You need to find out such things as:

- How long will the test be?
- What tools, equipment, etc., will be provided and what will you need to take with you?
- Can any preparatory work be done prior to the test?
- What will you be asked to create?
- How will the result be marked? e.g. by how quickly you did it? by how creative you were? by how accurate you were?

Then the critical thing is to practise again and again under these conditions. For example, you may be very good at producing paintings in six hours but have to sit an exam which gives you four hours. If you continue always to allow yourself six hours, you will not produce your best in a four-hour exam. You have therefore to concentrate on completing test pieces within a strict four-hour deadline. This type of practice pacing is essential for all timed practical tests.

You will not be able to produce work of the quality that you want when you first attempt a timed practice, so at the deadline you should stop and assess:

- How did you split up the available time? Too much on planning? Or on fine detail? Or on redoing parts where you were indecisive?
- Where/when did the work go well?
- Where/when did the work go badly?
- Did you try to over-perfect at any stage?
- Did your work ignore important marking criteria?

Then you can draw up a list of key points for tackling the next practice piece.

7.3   What are you asked to do?

Doing well in a test depends on doing what you are asked to do. Although tests are generally designed to let you show what you can do, it is also the case that you cannot generally get any credit for irrelevant answers. If you are asked to write about the causes of the First World War, you will get no marks for writing about the war itself. Reading the instructions for an assessment (called 'the rubric') as well as the precise wording of each question is therefore very important.

General instructions

You will find three crucial pieces of information in the general instructions:

- how much time you have;
- how many questions you have to answer;
- how the marks are distributed – or clues to this.

For example, in:

> 'Paper 1, 2½ hours. Answer all questions from section A and any two questions from section B'

the time is clear enough. It is also clear that you have no choice of what to answer in section A – all questions must be attempted. If you omit some questions from section A, you will not be able to make up for the lost marks by answering extra questions from section B. Finally, since you have a free choice of any two questions from section B, all section B questions must carry equal marks.

Activity 7.4   Looking for clues

Find an old assessment paper. Work out:

- how much time was allowed in total;
- how many questions had to be answered;
- where was choice possible?
- how were the marks distributed?
- what can you learn from the general instructions on the paper?

Question guidance

Most questions contain quite specific guidance on what sort of answer is required, for example:

- Explain with the aid of diagrams . . .
- List five ways . . .
- In short-answer format . . .
- Using quotations from . . .
- . . . in up to 200 words
- By reference to . . .
- Without the aid of a calculator . . .
- Give three examples of . . .
- Find . . . and hence solve . . .
- Find . . . and hence or otherwise solve . . .

These items are variously giving you hints and advice about:

- length;
- format;
- method;
- content.

Activity 7.5   Question guidance

Using an old assessment paper, find as many examples of guidance on length, format, method and content as you can. Identify for each what the guidance means in terms of what you must do and what you must not do.

Category	What you must do	What you must not do
Length examples		
Format examples		
Method examples		
Content examples		

7.4   Tactics

Doing your best in an assessment requires you to waste no effort. You have limited time and need to make every minute count.

Activity 7.6   Analysing your assessment tactics

For an assessment that you have recently taken, analyse what you did to:

Tactic	What you did
Choose which questions to answer	
Decide how much time to spend on each question	
Decide on how detailed each answer should be	

If you are happy that this strategy is highly effective for you, then stick to it. If not, the following ideas may help you.

Choosing your questions

Start the assessment by using the first few minutes to plan how you are going to tackle it. Read through all the questions and:

- Put a tick against those that you know you can answer reasonably well.
- Put a cross against those that you are certain it is not worth your while attempting.
- Put a question mark against the others.

If you can answer the required number of questions using only ticked questions, then do that.

If you have not ticked enough questions to complete the paper, you will need to answer a mixture of ticked and 'question-marked' questions. Clearly you are going to gain most of your marks from the ticked questions. Balancing your time to achieve this is discussed next.

Deciding on the time for each question

You need to work this out very carefully since a miscalculation could prove a severe handicap. For example, compare the following three separate approaches to the same assessment of five questions which had to be answered in two hours.

Question number	Method A Equal time for all questions	Method B Concentration on 1 and 2	Method C Use all time on 1 to 4
1	24 min	35 min	30 min
2	24 min	35 min	30 min
3	24 min	$16\,^2/_3$ min	30 min
4	24 min	$16\,^2/_3$ min	30 min
5	24 min	$16\,^2/_3$ min	—
TOTAL	120 min	120 min	120 min

The first approach, *A*, is what most people will aim for. But if you were to spend an extra ten minutes on each of the first two questions (method *B*), you automatically cut the time for the remaining questions to less than twenty minutes each. Worse (Method *C*), if you run over on the first four questions by only six minutes each, you have no time at all to start question 5.

So, in deciding on timing, you need to consider whether to:

- spend the same time on each question?
- spend less than the average time on your best questions? (Because you know them so well that you can quickly produce excellent answers.)
- spend more time than average on your best questions? (Because you will increase your overall mark in that way.)

Activity 7.7   Planning your time

Take an old assessment paper. Plan the distribution of your time over the questions.

Decide on the order

The question order is closely related to that of using your time well. Your choice is to answer in:

- the order on the paper
- your best questions first
- your worst questions first
- some other personal order.

Activity 7.8   How you use your time

In what order do you generally tackle the questions in an assessment? Does this order work well for you?

In general, the safest order is to answer your best questions first, perhaps spending a little extra time on them, but making sure that you leave enough time to answer the other questions as well as you can. There is a simple arithmetic explanation for this advice.

Suppose that you have to answer five questions. Two you know perfectly, two well enough to gain 75 per cent of their marks and one well enough to gain 30 per cent of its marks. If the total marks available are 100, the maximum that you can hope to get is:

Q1	100% of 20	=	20
Q2	100% of 20	=	20
Q3	75% of 20	=	15
Q4	75% of 20	=	15
Q5	30% of 20	=	6
TOTAL			76%

This clearly demonstrates the importance of spending enough time on the questions which you know best – probably allowing a little more than the average time for them. But the table also shows how even on a question about which you know little, six marks are there to be gained. So even your worst questions deserve enough time to extract what you can from them.

Decide on the detail

Again, detail is connected to time. The more time that you spend, the more detailed you can be. Should you give this detail?

The answer is 'No' for the same reason as not spending all your time on your best questions. A question designed to be answered in 24 minutes can be answered in 24 minutes and gain you its full marks. Adding more detail will take more time but there will be no extra marks. It is always important to recognise when your answer is good enough and at that point to move straight on to the next question.

If despite the best planning, you do run short of time, then do not panic. There is always the magic of a sketchy answer. Suppose that you are short of time – say you have ten minutes for a 24-minute answer – then it pays to sketch in just ten minutes the full answer that you would have given in 24 minutes. In just ten minutes, you can probably jot down all the key points or steps that you would have put into the answer and so perhaps gain over half the marks for the question. Working more slowly on a fully developed answer would gain far fewer marks in the same time.

Postscript

If you have read through this book, I hope that you have enjoyed it but I dare not hope that it has done much for your study skills. If you have worked through this book then I have great hopes for what you will achieve.

First, I hope that you found within yourself and your methods of working lots of points of success and many effective strategies. Much of this book has been designed to help you reflect on how you study so that you can build on what works for you.

Second, I hope that you are not too upset by the limited range of instant solutions and prescriptions in this book. You will know by now that I do not believe that they exist. Study is not easy even when you work at it effectively and efficiently.

Third, I hope that you have found that the process of reflecting on how you learn – your successes and failures – yields valuable insights from which you can make further improvements in your techniques. It is a skill worth keeping alive. To help you do that, here is one last activity, but one with a difference. It is not for use now but for occasional use at the end of any day – not just a day of formal study.

Activity 7.9 How did you learn today?

This activity is designed for use at the end of a day – the nearer the end the better. It is important to write down the answers to the questions since this will reinforce the messages that the activity gives you.

Remember 'learn' here refers to all your life, not just to study.

Make a list of everything which you learnt today. For each item, list:

- how you learnt it (e.g. by trial and error, by rote, through experience);
- what you did which made the learning more effective;
- what you did which hindered the learning.

Finally, complete the sentence:

- My learning today was a success because . . .

Appendices

Appendix A

Twenty words

table
car
music
Alice
door
sex
boot
bowl
bell
encyclopaedia
cup
hill
Peter
word
wear
loud
lamp
late
book
spoon

Appendix B

Twenty words

chair
van
song
Cathy
window

wealth
shoe
plate
plane
pomegranate

mug
date
John
letter
tear

noise
bulb
time
pen
fork

Index